PROMISE KEEPERS®
MEN OF INTEGRITY

PROMISE BUILDERS™
— STUDY SERIES —

CHARACTER
UNDER
CONSTRUCTION

WORD PUBLISHING

NASHVILLE

A Thomas Nelson Company

Printed in the United States of America
99 00 01 02 03 04 QPV 9 8 7 6 5 4 3 2 1

CONTENTS

FOREWORD

The subject of character is a hot topic these days; and, depending upon whom you talk to, what you read, or what poll you acknowledge, a variety of questions surfaces. Does the inner character of a person affect one's performance? Does character affect one's decision-making ability? Does it affect one's leadership? Are there absolutes that define what is right or wrong?

Polls consistently say that most people believe that public leaders should no longer be rated on virtues like honesty, fidelity, morality, humility, courage, prudence, and convictions. Rather, their character and moral leadership, say the majority in the polls, should be rated on services like improving education, building roads, aiding farmers, caring for the elderly, fighting crime, and feeding hungry children. Compassionate social services are certainly valuable to any society, but something is wrong with a society that does not see a connection between one's internal character and one's leadership.

Now, you may think that recent polls reflect the moral condition of the secular society, not the church at large. I, too, had hoped that this was the case. However, recently I heard some disturbing statistics at a George Barna seminar. When the Barna Research Center interviewed Christians and non-Christians about sixty-six lifestyle categories (such as what kind of entertainment they watch, whether they cheat on income taxes, whether they steal office supplies from their employer, whether they had sexual relations outside of their marriage, etc.), the Christians were not demonstrably different in even one category!

Yes, there is a problem with character, and the problem is not just "out there" in the world. It's "in here" too—in the church. I don't know about you, but the whole issue of integrity and character stops me in my tracks and causes me to ask God for mercy, for grace, and for power and strength to walk with Him faithfully—day in and day out. Without His presence in my life, I'm just another casualty to the world's and the enemy's ways of thinking and living.

I've known Bob Horner and Dave Sunde for nearly six years. We go to the same church, where they have taught from the pulpit and in Sunday school classes. They have written other books for Promise Keepers, and Bob has emceed numerous men's conferences. Together, they have more than fifty years' experience of discipling others in Christ.

When I was recently sick and on a sabbatical for five months, they consistently connected with me, taking me out for breakfasts just because they cared for me and my family. In the same way, I have observed them caring for their wives and children. They always seem to be talking about the things that matter to God—something godly men just do unconsciously. They aren't perfect (but neither am I, nor are you). But these guys are the real deal, the genuine article. They love God. They love their families. They love to disciple others to follow Christ. They are living examples of what I want to become. (And besides, Bob taught me how to fly-fish years ago, so I'm really indebted to him.) You'll enjoy the insight into the Scriptures that Dave and Bob bring.

Whether the polls believe it or not, absolutes do exist. Those absolutes are found in the holy, inspired Word of God. I pray that as you and other brothers in your small group go through *Character Under Construction,* the character of Christ will be constructed in you.

Pete Richardson
VP Communication Services
Promise Keepers

ACKNOWLEDGMENTS

Promise Keepers gives praise to our faithful Lord, Jesus Christ, for providing the talents and resources necessary to create this Promise Builders small-group study. We continue to be amazed at the grace the Lord extends to this ministry. With deep gratitude, we wish to acknowledge:

- Bob Horner and Dave Sunde, who shared their creative minds and wrote the studies to spur men on to greater growth in Christ. We are grateful for the time they gave to test and solidify the material with existing small groups.

- Pete Richardson, Mary Guenther, Todd McMullen, and Tracey D. Lawrence from Promise Keepers.

- Laura Kendall from Word Publishing and Jennifer Stair, who edited this book.

Also, we are thankful to you, the reader, who encourages us to continue publishing resources for men's ministry.

INTRODUCTION

Our title, *Character Under Construction*, implies that our character can change. This is good news. None of us wants to be stuck in the rut of our past, with its sins, mistakes, and wrong decisions. But how does our character change? It changes one biblical insight at a time, one decision at a time, one day at a time. The patterns of the past are gradually replaced with the new principles and insights we are learning from the Bible. However, the goal is not perfection; it is change according to the pattern of Jesus Christ. He loves us too much to leave us in our sin and separation from Almighty God. His death for us accomplished that. Now, as our new life is centered in Him, we can anticipate wonderful changes in our character. Our life will be increasingly described by the fruit of the Holy Spirit: a cluster of qualities that we may never have thought possible. Imagine being described by your family, friends, and associates as loving, kind, loyal, patient, joyful, and self-controlled!

Our character defines who we really are. We must remember that we bring who we really are to all the areas of our lives. Our leadership, our family life, and even our financial matters and decisions are included in our character. We will focus on each of these areas, one at a time, as we meet in the weeks of our study and interaction together. Twelve sessions on each area are designed to develop the growth of your character in the power of the Holy Spirit. As mentioned above, the intent of each session is to make discoveries in God's timeless Word to us, the Bible. There will be suggested ways to apply those insights immediately. As the apostle Peter instructed, "Grow in the grace and knowledge of our Lord and Savior Jesus Christ" (2 Peter 3:18).

Growth in our character as individuals will make its mark on the world around us, even as Jesus anticipated. We will be salt and light in a world greatly in need of illumination and preservation of the truth. As economist Roger W. Babson said, "A character standard is far more important than a gold standard. The success of all economic systems is still dependent upon both righteous leaders and righteous people. In the last analysis, our national future depends upon our national character—that is, whether it is spiritually or materially minded." *Character Under Construction* aims at changing us into spiritually minded men in the months ahead. Now is the time to make our mark as godly men.

Bob Horner
David Sunde
Boulder, CO

THE BEST APPROACH FOR YOUR GROUP

AN OVERVIEW OF SEVERAL PATTERNS OF MEN'S SMALL-GROUP BIBLE STUDIES

Men who gather in a small group to fellowship, study the Bible, and pray together predictably follow one of several patterns. Often they aren't even aware of what their group has become, since they're accustomed to it. Of course, the leader of the group has tremendous influence in this area. The kind of group we have in mind for these sessions may call for some changes in the way your group does things (if yours is an established group). But we hope you'll see the benefits of becoming a group that majors in interactive discussion and application of the timeless insights of God's Word.

"Adrift"
THE LIFE RAFT GROUP

This small group is made up of survivors—men who have survived a major battle in their lives. It may have been a recent battle or one from years ago. But the wounds and scars are reminders of what each has suffered. What began as an emergency situation has turned into a weekly meeting. So each man is just happy to be among his friends. Life raft groups really have no leader—each man has his own story to tell around some biblical idea or paragraph. Of concern to the men is that they're adrift. And though high on encouragement, they're low on long-term biblical resources.

"Feeling Good"
THE YACHT GROUP

If you long to feel good among friends, climb aboard this craft! The skipper will welcome you with a hot cup of coffee or whatever else you'd like. Each man needs a Bible, of course—and the study will begin as soon as they push off. But meanwhile, they'll just enjoy the Lord and one another. For some reason, the seagoing stories of fellow mariners always take more time than the skipper planned for, so time in the Word will resume next week. Your need to move beyond the fellowship—to get into the Word—may urge you on to see what other boats are in the harbor.

"Battle Weary"
THE DESTROYER GROUP

This pattern is named after the naval vessel of the same class. It's a warship, armed and ready for battle against the forces of evil in society and our lives. Disciplined Bible study is the order of the day. Truth from Scripture is fired from the leader like missiles from the deck launchers. Some of the sailors look as if they have taken direct hits from the Word, but the leader has properly warned them that such are the costs of discipleship. No one questions the reality of spiritual warfare, though the battle-weary men sense the need for some spiritual support from the Lord.

"Deep and Long: Where Are We?"
THE SUBMARINE GROUP

To the captain of the sub, there are just two kinds of boats: subs and targets. Aboard this kind of small group, Bible study gives the experience of going down deep, staying down long, and, after a while, wondering where you really are. A life of disciplined study is essential if you're to last with this group. And you may not be sure the captain likes you, but you know you're investing time in a highly strategic activity below the surface of life. If it's fellowship balanced with interactive Bible study and prayer you're looking for, however, you'd better not go down the ladder into the sub group.

"Refreshed, Refueled, Refocused"
THE CARRIER GROUP

An aircraft carrier is a warship equipped with a large open deck for the taking off and landing of warplanes. As well, it's equipped to carry, service, and arm its planes. A small-group Bible study in this pattern is on a mission, under way to be in strategic position for the men on board. Each time the men come in, in the midst of the workweek, they know they will be refreshed, refueled, and refocused for life's battles and open seas. They leave ready to fulfill the biblical plan they studied, alert to serve their Captain well. This kind of small group is what we have in mind for the sessions ahead. Of course there is value in the other kinds of group patterns, but we believe that the aircraft carrier model best serves our goal of becoming Promise Builders in the year before us.

LEADER'S GUIDELINES

This book contains forty-eight sessions of Bible studies for your small group plus a special lesson for Christmas—a year's supply. It is anticipated that your group will meet weekly except for unforeseen situations unique to your group.

Each weekly session is designed to take one hour. The questions for each session are answered interactively in the group. The opening **ten minutes** are for fellowship around coffee and friendship. Then allow **forty minutes** to interact with the biblical material. Use the final **ten minutes** for application and prayer. A small clock icon in each study will remind you to set aside those ten minutes. A special **Prayer Journal** is provided to record the various requests week by week.

Leaders of small-group Bible studies have traditionally been people of superior biblical knowledge and (hopefully) great spiritual maturity. But in Promise Builders small groups, we're changing some of the rules. Our leaders are meant to be facilitators, not biblical experts. The purpose of the Promise Builder group leader is to encourage discussion and interaction. Thus, he is more a coach than a commentator. In other words, the group is meant to be leader-light.

There are, however, a few other responsibilities for the leader:

- Start and end each session on time. This shows respect for the men and their work schedules.

- Pray for group members by name before each meeting.

- Value each man's comments and insights.

- Secure a meeting place, preferably in the marketplace rather than a home or church—someplace like the back of a restaurant, a cafeteria, a conference room, a community center, or someone's office.

- Work closely with the men who are facilitating the group in other ways, such as the timekeeper, the prayer leader, and the calendar coordinator.

- Note that there is a special session for the Christmas season.

Following these simple guidelines, plus the *carrier-group* mind-set described in the Best Approach for Your Group, will help you and the other men in your group see life-changing results as you go through the studies in this book.

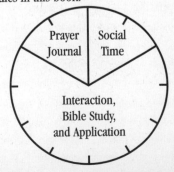

CHARACTER UNDER CONSTRUCTION

A PROVEN WAY TO BE A MAN OF GODLY CHARACTER AT WORK, AT HOME, AND IN FINANCIAL MATTERS

Benjamin Franklin once said, "He who shall introduce into public affairs the principles of primitive [original] Christianity will change the face of the world." The challenge before us is to be men of Christlike character, men who embrace biblical values of honesty and diligence, men whose handshake is as good as the most carefully worded contract. Men like this are in short supply today in the homes and workplaces of our nation.

This is our opportunity to "change the face of the world"! The goal of this study is to experience character transformation so that we can be world-changers. A proven way to become a godly man and have such influence is to follow a plan that progresses through four concentric circles. Of course, no plan has the power to change anyone's life; only as we are filled with the Holy Spirit will change take place. But the Spirit of God can work in our lives through a plan that is centered in the Lord and His Word. This is exactly how the sessions and weeks of this study are arranged. As you move progressively through the weeks of study and interaction, the Holy Spirit is advancing you through the circles. An equipping process is under way, so you can express your character and values that

are God-honoring and meaningful in a world of compromise and expedience.

The core circle: *Walk*. The goal in this section of studies is to equip you in the basics of a daily relationship with Jesus Christ. We're calling it your *walk* with the Lord. A meaningful and growing *walk* will be centered in God's Word. That's the primary way He speaks to us. If we're to have a quality *walk* with Him, we need to communicate with Him daily. So prayer is the next focus of study. Finally, the power to achieve God's will, as discovered in the Word and in prayer, comes from the Holy Spirit. It's essential that we're rightly related to His powerful presence within us. The beginning of our impact for Christ is in our daily *walk* with Him.

The second circle: *Work*. Building a good reputation in the workplace, at home, and in our finances has everything to do with the quality of our *work* performance in these areas. In this section of Bible studies, the goal is to equip you in both your perspective on and your attitude toward *work*.

The third circle: *Relationships.* The good news of Jesus Christ travels on the network of *relationships* in the workplace, at home, and virtually everywhere we go. We need to follow biblical guidelines for winning friends and influencing people on the job. Naturally, we'll have to overcome some barriers to make good *relationships* a part of our work life and home life. But whatever it takes to build a bridge to those with whom you work and live, you'll be doing what Jesus would do if He were in your shoes.

The fourth circle: *Ministry.* People need the Lord. The marketplace, and other places people gather, are areas of opportunity to bring the Light of Jesus Christ. How will our fellow workers, even family members and friends in the neighborhood, ever hear of new life in Jesus? Our great opportunity is to introduce them to Him. But that's just the beginning! We can also help new Christians grow in the Lord and become a part of the church. Our prayer is that as you go through these studies with your small group you'll be both equipped and motivated to take up the challenge of being a man whose character is under construction. Then you will be helping to change the face of the world for God's glory.

Mission Statement

Promise Keepers is a Christ-centered ministry dedicated to uniting men through vital relationships to become godly influences in their world.

The Seven Promises

OF A PROMISE KEEPER

❶ A man and his God.
A Promise Keeper is committed to honor Jesus Christ through worship, prayer, and obedience to His Word in the power of the Holy Spirit.

❷ A man and his friends.
A Promise Keeper is committed to pursuing vital relationships with a few other men, understanding that he needs brothers to help him keep his promises.

❸ A man and his integrity.
A Promise Keeper is committed to practicing spiritual, moral, ethical, and sexual purity.

❹ A man and his family.
A Promise Keeper is committed to build a strong marriage and family through love, protection, and biblical values.

❺ A man and his church.
A Promise Keeper is committed to support the mission of his church by honoring and praying for his pastors and actively giving his time and resources.

❻ A man and his brothers.
A Promise Keeper is committed to reach beyond any racial and denominational barriers to demonstrate the power of biblical unity.

❼ A man and his world.
A Promise Keeper is committed to influencing his world, being obedient to the Great Commandment (Mark 12:30–31) and the Great Commission (Matthew 28:19–20).

BUILDING INSPECTION

FIRST IN A SERIES OF THREE STUDIES:
CHARACTER IS DEVELOPED IN OUR WALK

CHARACTER TRAIT UNDER CONSTRUCTION: A SOLID FOUNDATION

• •

WARM-UP: THEY SEE THE CONSTRUCTION EVERY DAY. IT SEEMS THE STRUCTURE IS TAKING FOREVER TO FINISH. SOMEONE IN THE CARPOOL ASKS, "ARE THEY EVER GOING TO GET THAT BUILDING UP?" ANOTHER RESPONDS WITH, "I SUPPOSE IT MUST TAKE A LOT OF WORK TO BUILD A STRUCTURE OF THAT SIZE!" TALK TOGETHER OF WHAT MIGHT HAPPEN IF THE CONSTRUCTION COMPANY TOOK SHORTCUTS IN THIS PROJECT.

BACKGROUND

In this first of twelve sessions, we will discover *Character Under Construction*. Our starting point is to consider how to build our lives and character. In the apostle Paul's day, strife in the church at Corinth was evidence that the Corinthians were building with inferior materials. We have the same challenge today. Will we build our lives and character wisely? When God begins to build in our lives, He always starts with the foundation.

(WALK) ⇒

A SOLID FOUNDATION

READ

1 CORINTHIANS 3:9–15

QUESTIONS FOR INTERACTION:

❶ The apostle Paul states that Jesus Christ is the only foundation for life and character. Why?

❷ Why does Paul alert us to the dangers of taking shortcuts while building on this solid foundation?

❸ Compare and contrast the building materials available for life and character.

4 Describe a Christian you know (no names necessary) whose life and character reflect the right building materials.

REPUTATION IS WHAT PEOPLE THINK YOU ARE.

CHARACTER IS WHAT YOU REALLY ARE.

5 At the building site, the workers are uneasy when they see the periodic arrival of the building inspector's truck. Why should we also have a certain uneasiness about Judgment Day?

WRAP-UP: UNFORESEEN CHALLENGES IN OUR LIVES HAVE A WAY OF INSPECTING OUR CHARACTER-BUILDING PROCESS. TALK TOGETHER OF RECENT CHALLENGES THAT HAVE CONFRONTED MEMBERS OF THE GROUP.

LET'S PRAY:

ONE MINUTE: PRAY SILENTLY ABOUT TODAY'S STUDY
TWO MINUTES: EXPRESS THANKS TO GOD TOGETHER
THREE MINUTES: WRITE IN YOUR PRAYER JOURNAL
FOUR MINUTES: PRAY FOR EACH OTHER

MY RESPONSE AS A PROMISE KEEPER

1 I will ask the Lord to examine my character using Psalm 139:23–24.

2 I will begin making the necessary adjustments He reveals.

HOURS IN THE SHOWER

SECOND IN A SERIES OF THREE STUDIES:
CHARACTER IS DEVELOPED IN OUR WALK

CHARACTER TRAIT UNDER CONSTRUCTION: PURITY

• •

WARM-UP: FILM WRITERS OFTEN LET THEIR VIEWERS HEAR THE SHOWER RUNNING AFTER A SCENE OF IMMORALITY. THESE WRITERS ARE RELYING ON THE PSYCHOLOGICAL PREMISE THAT PEOPLE WHO ARE OVERCOME BY GUILT SOMEHOW THINK A SHOWER CAN MAKE THEM CLEAN. SINCE IMMORALITY IS SO COMMONPLACE THESE DAYS, DISCUSS TOGETHER WHY THERE IS SUCH A NEED TO EXPERIENCE GENUINE CLEANSING FROM THE GUILT.

BACKGROUND

The story is quite well-known: a powerful king, an attractive woman, a choice, a "shower." Two chapters in the Old Testament describe David's breach of character (2 Sam. 11–12). In today's session in the Psalms, we will uncover the rest of the story.

READ

PSALM 51:1-13

QUESTIONS FOR INTERACTION:

❶ How could King David, known for his godly character, run after Bathsheba with unbridled lust?

❷ Talk together of the gut-wrenching turmoil that came into David's life following adultery. Why was this so painful?

WALK ⇒

PURITY

❸ Who was hurt by David's sin? Then why would he tell God, "Against you, you only have I sinned" (v. 4)?

4 If David had not chosen to repent, what would have happened to his heart?

5 Based on this psalm, describe the heart of the person who highly values moral purity.

WRAP-UP: KING DAVID'S CHARACTER WAS UNDER CONSTRUCTION ONCE AGAIN. TOGETHER, LIST REASONS WHY A HOLY GOD CONTINUES TO HELP US BUILD MORAL PURITY IN OUR CHARACTER.

 LET'S PRAY: (SEE PRAYER JOURNAL)

• •

MY RESPONSE AS A PROMISE KEEPER

❶ I will repent and not resist God's inspection of my life and character.

❷ I will pray for myself and the other members of my group to maintain moral purity.

BEYOND BARBELLS

THIRD IN A SERIES OF THREE STUDIES:
CHARACTER IS DEVELOPED IN OUR WALK

CHARACTER TRAIT UNDER CONSTRUCTION: GODLINESS

• •

WARM-UP: OUR CULTURE IS OBSESSED WITH BUILDING BUNS OF STEEL AND WASHBOARD ABS. BUT, WE ALL KNOW THAT WHEN WE PURCHASE FITNESS EQUIPMENT, IT OFTEN ENDS UP BEING SOLD AT GARAGE SALES. TALK TOGETHER ABOUT WHY WE ARE SO SUSCEPTIBLE TO BUYING THIS STUFF.

BACKGROUND

READ

1 TIMOTHY 4:1–16

Two letters in the New Testament bear the name of Timothy, who was the star student of the great apostle Paul. As Timothy's mentor, Paul worked hard to guide Timothy into building a life of godly character. This godly character is at the heart of our study today.

QUESTIONS FOR INTERACTION:

1 A life of godliness will always be surrounded by strange teachings, godless myths, and man-made religions. Describe examples you have witnessed.

2 Why do you think Paul was so forceful in warning Timothy to steer clear of these teachings?

WALK ⇨

GODLINESS

3 Why do we often associate godliness with people who are much older than we are?

PROMISE
KEEPERS®
MEN OF INTEGRITY

④ Paul tells his young disciple, "Train yourself to be godly" (v. 7). What does Paul say should be Timothy's exercise program?

⑤ Agree/Disagree: We should give less time to working out physically than we do to maintaining spiritual fitness. Why/Why not?

WRAP-UP:

WHETHER WE ARE TALKING ABOUT SPIRITUAL FITNESS OR PHYSICAL FITNESS, THERE WILL BE BARRIERS. <u>DISCUSS TOGETHER</u> WHAT YOU HAVE FOUND TO BE BARRIERS TO EACH.

LET'S PRAY: (SEE PRAYER JOURNAL)

● ●

MY RESPONSE AS A PROMISE KEEPER

❶ I will begin my spiritual fitness program by exercising with _____ (suggested exercises include: Bible study, prayer, and fellowship)

❷ Knowing that godly character is more than a set of activities, I will review my relationship with Christ and ask the Holy Spirit to refresh my relationship with Him.

KICK THE "L" OUT OF GOLD

FIRST IN THE SERIES OF THREE STUDIES:
CHARACTER IS EXAMINED IN OUR WORK

CHARACTER TRAIT UNDER CONSTRUCTION: CONTENTMENT

• •

WARM-UP:
THIS WEEK THE STATE LOTTERY JACKPOT IS UP TO $13 MILLION. CONVERSATION IN THE WORKPLACE AND IN FITNESS CLUBS CENTERS AROUND THE QUESTION, "HOW MANY TICKETS ARE YOU GOING TO BUY?" THE HOPE OF BECOMING AN INSTANT MILLIONAIRE HAS GRABBED NEARLY EVERYONE'S ATTENTION. DISCUSS TOGETHER WHY THERE IS SUCH A LONGING IN MILLIONS OF PEOPLE TO BE RICH.

BACKGROUND

Somewhere in this letter to young Timothy the apostle Paul knows he must deal with the lust to be rich. He knows there are few things that destroy character faster than the desire to be wealthy. He doesn't waste words, but goes directly to the heart of the matter to "kick the 'L' out of GoLd."

READ

1 TIMOTHY 6:3–11

QUESTIONS FOR INTERACTION:

1 The apostle Paul is quick to say that love of God and love of gold do not mix. Why does this tension exist?

2 However, godliness and contentment do mix well. Why is this combination without tension?

3 Why do you think "the love of money is a root of all kinds of evil" (v. 10)?

CONTENTMENT

④ According to Paul, what happens to the person who works and lives to make a lot of money?

⑤ If the goal of making money will not bring contentment, what will?

WRAP-UP: TALK TOGETHER ABOUT PEOPLE YOU KNOW WHO HAVE LOST MUCH BECAUSE THEY DIDN'T HEED THE WARNING OF TODAY'S SCRIPTURE.

 LET'S PRAY: (SEE PRAYER JOURNAL)

● ●

MY RESPONSE AS A PROMISE KEEPER

❶ I will ask myself, "Am I content?" If not, is it because of my love for gold?

❷ I will take seriously the apostle's warning regarding the love of gold by listing my current priorities to see where they fall in light of pursuing godly character.

Return to a Good Reputation

Second in the series of three studies: Character Is Examined in Our WORK

Character Trait Under Construction: GOOD REPUTATION

● ●

WARM-UP: It is often said, "His reputation goes before him." Notable success often results in noteworthy reputation. Sometimes the opposite is true. Talk together of examples of both good and bad reputations. (Suggested personalities: Sam Walton, Ted Turner, Pete Rose, Bill Gates)

BACKGROUND

Even though his name meant "useful," Onesimus ran away from Philemon, his employer. But God had a plan for Onesimus that included meeting and being mentored by the great apostle Paul. Paul knew that character is the cornerstone of reputation, and he communicated this truth to Onesimus. The question before us today is why Philemon should rehire a man of formerly poor reputation.

READ

PHILEMON 1–25

Questions for Interaction:

1 What kind of reputation did Onesimus have with Philemon, his employer, when he ran away?

2 Onesimus was not only a runaway employee, he also may have stolen from Philemon. Why do you think Paul would associate with such a disreputable person?

3 How do you think Onesimus must have changed so that he moved from being "useless" to "useful" both to Paul and to Philemon?

WALK → WORK

GOOD REPUTATION

PROMISE KEEPERS®
MEN OF INTEGRITY

4 Why do we, along with Philemon, have a very difficult time changing our minds about the previous poor reputation of a former employee?

5 Why do you think this unusual and brief letter is included in the New Testament?

WRAP-UP: OUR PASSAGE FOR STUDY DOESN'T SAY WHETHER PHILEMON REHIRED ONESIMUS. YOUR GROUP IS HIS EMPLOYEE REVIEW COMMITTEE. DISCUSS TOGETHER WHETHER YOU WOULD REHIRE THIS FORMER EMPLOYEE.

 LET'S PRAY: (SEE PRAYER JOURNAL)

• •

MY RESPONSE AS A PROMISE KEEPER

❶ I will pray for the return of a good reputation for _____, who used to work with/for me.

❷ I will ask a close friend at work to help me evaluate my workplace reputation.

HARD WORK IN HARD TIMES

CHARACTER TRAIT UNDER CONSTRUCTION: **WORKING HARD**

• •

WARM-UP:

CARL WORKS AS AN AUTOMOTIVE ENGINEER IN THE MIDWESTERN UNITED STATES. HE HAS BEEN WITH THE SAME COMPANY FOR SIXTEEN YEARS. CARL IS BEGINNING TO DREAD MONDAYS, AND HE IS INCREASINGLY NEGATIVE THE REST OF THE WORKWEEK. <u>DISCUSS TOGETHER</u> WHAT MIGHT BE MAKING CARL'S WORK LIFE SO HARD AND UNBEARABLE.

BACKGROUND

Working hard is evidence of good character. The one who is the focus of our session today was a hard worker. Therefore, God was able to entrust to a man named Noah the most challenging task given to a person of his time.

READ

GENESIS 5:28–29; 6:5–22

QUESTIONS FOR INTERACTION:

1 What was work like during the days of Noah and his father?

2 Agree/Disagree. Noah would never be elected as head of the local Carpenters Union. Why/Why not?

3 We sometimes think that leaving a secular job and working in ministry would make our work life so much more meaningful. What do you think Noah might say to this kind of reasoning?

WALK WORK ⇨

WORKING HARD

4 In what ways might Noah's ability to work hard have affected his workweek?

5 What does Noah teach us about making work meaningful as God intended it?

WRAP-UP: DISCUSS TOGETHER SOMETHING THAT TO YOU IS WORKING HARD BUT IS NOT NECESSARILY HARD WORK. WHY?

LET'S PRAY: (SEE PRAYER JOURNAL)

· ·

MY RESPONSE AS A PROMISE KEEPER

1 I will try to see my work as Noah saw his: working for God.

2 I will resist complaining about hard work and working hard.

FIDO FACES FURY

● ●

WARM-UP:
IT WAS JUST ANOTHER DAY, I THOUGHT. I GOBBLED DOWN MY GRAVY TRAIN. I TOOK A NAP. I CLEARED THE YARD OF TWO PESKY CATS. BUT, LATER THAT AFTERNOON, WHILE NAPPING BY THE BACK DOOR, I WAS BRUTALLY AWAKENED BY A SHARP KICK TO MY RIBS. "OH NO, MY MASTER HAD ANOTHER BAD DAY AT THE OFFICE!" DISCUSS TOGETHER WHAT MIGHT CONTRIBUTE TO FIDO'S ALLEGIANCE TO HIS MASTER.

BACKGROUND

The setting for the study today is Moab (modern-day Jordan). This nation's religious system was the exact opposite of the worship of the true God. We men have so much to learn about *relationships* from women. Today we will meet three widows who had no Social Security and no life insurance benefits. We will discover from one of these widows how hard times actually reveal character, especially in relationships.

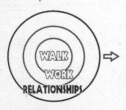

COMMITMENT

READ

RUTH 1:1–22

QUESTIONS FOR INTERACTION:

❶ What hard times did Naomi face? What did these hard times reveal about her character?

❷ How do you think Naomi's trip to Moab affected her view of God?

❸ Why do you think Ruth was so committed to Naomi?

4 Ruth's commitment was to a disheartened and disillusioned mother-in-law. What did Ruth's commitment do for Naomi?

WRAP-UP: RUTH EXPRESSED INCREDIBLE COMMITMENT TO HER MOTHER-IN-LAW. HAVE EACH PERSON IN THE GROUP THINK OF A CHALLENGING RELATIONSHIP HE HAS. <u>DISCUSS TOGETHER</u> WHAT RUTH TEACHES US MEN ABOUT WHAT MIGHT MAKE THAT RELATIONSHIP STRONGER.

 LET'S PRAY

ONE MINUTE: PRAY SILENTLY ABOUT TODAY'S STUDY
TWO MINUTES: EXPRESS THANKS TO GOD TOGETHER
THREE MINUTES: WRITE IN YOUR PRAYER JOURNAL
FOUR MINUTES: PRAY FOR EACH OTHER

MY RESPONSE AS A PROMISE KEEPER

❶ I will reread this chapter with the person in mind who needs my commitment.

❷ I will express words of commitment to the person I identified in the Wrap-Up.

BOTHERED BY BALL CAPS

SECOND IN THE SERIES OF THREE STUDIES:
CHARACTER IS TESTED IN OUR **RELATIONSHIPS**

CHARACTER TRAIT UNDER CONSTRUCTION: **GIVING RESPECT**

● ●

WARM-UP:

PLAYING THE NATIONAL ANTHEM IS AN OPPORTUNITY FOR FANS TO SHOW RESPECT FOR THE NATION AND HER FLAG. THE ROW OF HIGH SCHOOL BOYS STANDING IN FRONT OF YOU DO NOT REMOVE THEIR BALL CAPS. THIS BOTHERS YOU. <u>DISCUSS TOGETHER</u> WHAT YOU WOULD DO IN THIS SITUATION.

BACKGROUND

In our previous session, we followed Ruth and Naomi out of the land of Moab to Israel. Ruth's character revealed strong commitment in a challenging in-law relationship. In today's session, we will see another facet of her character under construction. In the setting of her rural workplace, Ruth will model for us men a rare respect for the one who gave her working privileges.

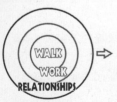

GIVING RESPECT

PROMISE KEEPERS®
MEN OF INTEGRITY

READ

RUTH 2:1–16

QUESTIONS FOR INTERACTION:

1 In what ways did Ruth show respect for Naomi? Why do you think she related to her mother-in-law this way?

2 How can we tell that Ruth felt deep respect for Naomi's people? What were the benefits to Ruth of showing respect to Boaz?

3 Obviously, Boaz was impressed by Ruth. What likely contributed to this?

4 In the rural workplace of that day, women were commonly mistreated. Often our places of work are not much different. Why?

5 Workers who are genuinely respectful and quick to serve are sometimes taken advantage of. How have you seen this demonstrated in the workplace?

WRAP-UP. A RESPECTFUL SPIRIT IS HIGHLY VALUED IN AN EMPLOYEE. <u>DISCUSS TOGETHER</u> HOW WE MIGHT SPOT THIS CHARACTER QUALITY IN SOMEONE BEFORE WE HIRE THEM.

LET'S PRAY: (SEE PRAYER JOURNAL)

• •

MY RESPONSE AS A PROMISE KEEPER

❶ I will seek to demonstrate my respect for those around me by

_____.

❷ I will encourage those who are respectful and quick to serve by

_____.

HEADS UP!

. . . .

WARM-UP:

BILL'S SENSE OF DIGNITY DOESN'T COME FROM HIS HOME LIFE. HOWEVER, GOING TO WORK DOES SOMETHING FOR HIM. IF YOU WERE HIS FELLOW EMPLOYEE, YOU WOULD THINK HIS HEAD WAS ALWAYS HIGH. DISCUSS TOGETHER WHAT COULD BE HAPPENING TO BILL WHEN HE ARRIVES AT WORK.

BACKGROUND

READ

Today, as we continue to focus on character tested in relationships, we will meet still another woman. She desperately needs what apparently no man in her culture would extend: dignity. Dignity was withheld from virtually every woman of her day. In this session, we will watch one man's uncharacteristic response to a woman.

LUKE 7:36–50

QUESTIONS FOR INTERACTION:

❶ Why do you suppose this Pharisee invited Jesus to dinner?

❷ Speculate for a moment about what this uninvited woman may have known about Jesus that would have motivated her to barge in on His dinner.

WALK
WORK
RELATIONSHIPS ⇨

GIVING DIGNITY

❸ Why do you think Simon was unable to give this woman any dignity?

4 How did Jesus give dignity to the woman?

5 What benefits came to the woman from being valued by Jesus?

WRAP-UP:
DESCRIBE PEOPLE WHO SEEM TO RECEIVE LITTLE DIGNITY FROM THOSE AROUND THEM IN THE WORKPLACE. DISCUSS TOGETHER WHAT BARRIERS PREVENT OTHERS FROM GIVING THEM DIGNITY.

 LET'S PRAY: (SEE PRAYER JOURNAL)

● ●

MY RESPONSE AS A PROMISE KEEPER

❶ I will determine who in my workplace needs to be seen as Jesus saw the woman: _____.

❷ I will extend dignity to this person by _____

_____.

(e.g., greeting by name, expressing appreciation for work done)

A Soldier's Psalm

● ●

WARM-UP: THE 1995 ACADEMY AWARD–WINNING BEST PICTURE WAS A BLOODY ONE. THE SCOTS FOUGHT FOR THE FREEDOM OF SCOTLAND AGAINST THE ENCROACHING POWER OF THE ENGLISH CROWN. "BRAVEHEART'S" LEAD WARRIOR WAS GRIPPED BY A PASSION TO SET HIS COUNTRYMEN FREE. DISCUSS TOGETHER HOW A PASSION IS BORN IN A PERSON. THEN DESCRIBE SOMEONE YOU KNOW WHO IS A PERSON OF PASSION.

BACKGROUND

One of King David's work responsibilities was to go to war. David saw himself as God's man on the battlefield, his workplace. And David was a passionate warrior. In today's session, we will seek to discover the passion that motivated his service for God at work.

READ

2 SAMUEL 21:15–22:4, 29–32

QUESTIONS FOR INTERACTION:

❶ In the midst of battle, General Patton said, "God, I love it!" King David, also a warrior, said, "God, I love You!" Whose army would you like to be in and why?

❷ How did David express his passion for God?

❸ What did David's passion for God do for him?

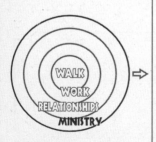

WALK
WORK
RELATIONSHIPS
MINISTRY

PASSION FOR GOD

4 Why do you think passion for God appears so infrequently in the workplace?

HARD HAT AREA:

"GOD, I LOVE IT!"

GENERAL PATTON

"GOD, I LOVE YOU!"

KING DAVID

5 David's world of work and passion for God were integrated. He said, "God is my rock . . . my stronghold, my refuge and my savior" (22:3). If your world of work and passion for God were integrated, choose words you might use to complete this statement: "God is my
_____."

WRAP-UP: IF YOUR PASSION FOR GOD WERE TO BE REVEALED IN YOUR SPHERE OF WORK, <u>DISCUSS TOGETHER</u> WHAT YOU WOULD LIKE PEOPLE TO SEE.

 LET'S PRAY: (SEE PRAYER JOURNAL)

· ·

MY RESPONSE AS A PROMISE KEEPER

1 I will give Him the first fifteen minutes of each workday this week to rekindle the passion.

2 I will be alert as to how my rekindled passion might be expressed at work.

"Do You See What I See?"

• •

WARM-UP:

LIKE A LOT OF US, JIM SAVORS BEING HOME ON SATURDAY MORNING. FINALLY, HE HAS SOME TIME TO WORK ON UNFINISHED PROJECTS INSIDE THE HOUSE OR OUTSIDE IN THE YARD. ABOUT HALF OF JIM'S YARD WORK IS COMPLETED, AND HE IS TAKING A BREAK IN THE SHADE. OUT OF THE CORNER OF HIS EYE HE SPOTS HIS PESKY NEIGHBOR HEADING HIS WAY. ALL OF US RESPOND TO INTERRUPTIONS LIKE THIS DIFFERENTLY. HAVE EACH GROUP MEMBER DESCRIBE WHAT HE WOULD LIKELY DO WITH THIS NEIGHBOR.

BACKGROUND

READ

There are many places in our session today where we could land: lessons in evangelism, overcoming racial barriers, and being sensitive to religious differences. However, our focus is to discover the character trait in Jesus that was so often expressed in His ministry: a heart for people.

JOHN 4:4–42

QUESTIONS FOR INTERACTION:

1 Jesus was tired from His journey, stopping to rest by Jacob's well. What was His response when His rest was interrupted?

2 Why was Jesus willing to get involved with this woman when He was so tired?

3 The disciples let Jesus rest at the well while they went to get food. When they returned, their response to this woman was different from Jesus' response. Why?

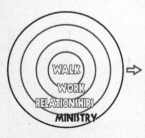

HEART FOR PEOPLE

PROMISE
KEEPERS®
MEN OF INTEGRITY

④ Why was Jesus more interested in people than food?

⑤ Jesus' heart for people caused Him to see them as a "harvest" (v. 35). What is the significance of His analogy?

WRAP-UP: IT IS EASY FOR US TO SEE PEOPLE AND JUST LOOK PAST THEM. WHAT WOULD BE THE BENEFITS OF SEEING PEOPLE AS JESUS DID? <u>DISCUSS AS A GROUP.</u>

LET'S PRAY: (SEE PRAYER JOURNAL)

MY RESPONSE AS A PROMISE KEEPER

❶ I will begin developing a heart for the people I see at work by praying for them.

❷ I will begin to view interruptions as possible invitations to minister.

What Is Mine Is Yours

Third in the series of three studies:
Character Is Expressed in Our MINISTRY
Character Trait Under Construction: COMPASSION

• •

WARM-UP: STANDING WITH HIS FAMILY IN CHURCH, BILL RECITES THE LORD'S PRAYER FERVENTLY, AS ALWAYS. FOLLOWING THE CHOIR'S PRESENTATION OF THE MORNING ANTHEM, AN ELDER IN CHARGE OF CHURCH OUTREACH SEEKS TO ENLIST WORKERS FOR AN INNER-CITY PROJECT. BILL WHISPERS TO HIS WIFE, "WHY DO THEY INTERRUPT OUR WORSHIP WITH SUCH PERIPHERAL APPEALS?" DISCUSS TOGETHER WHAT YOU LIKE OR DISLIKE ABOUT BILL'S RESPONSE.

BACKGROUND

Today we will meet a man whose character was clearly under construction. Although he was religious, he was about to discover a new dimension to his otherwise well-ordered life. As a lawyer, he knew how to ask good questions. The one question he raised to Jesus launched a story that has become known worldwide.

COMPASSION

READ

LUKE 10:25-37

QUESTIONS FOR INTERACTION:

1 Put together a personal profile of the lawyer Jesus met. Why do you think he wanted to "justify himself" (v. 29)?

2 How might we explain the religious professionals' (the priest and the Levite) feeling no compassion for the beaten-up stranger?

3 Where do you suppose the good Samaritan got his compassion for the victim?

4 Jews of that day despised Samaritans, who were half-breeds of Jews who intermarried with pagans. So why do you think Jesus made a Samaritan the hero in this story?

5 According to this story, what does compassion look like?

WRAP-UP:

HAVE EACH PERSON IN THE GROUP THINK OF A PERSON OF NEED IN HIS WORKPLACE. <u>DISCUSS TOGETHER</u> WHAT TENDS TO KEEP US FROM BEING COMPASSIONATE TOWARD THEM.

LET'S PRAY: (SEE PRAYER JOURNAL)

● ●

MY RESPONSE AS A PROMISE KEEPER

❶ I will pray specifically to become a person of greater compassion.

❷ I will seek to be a Good Samaritan to the person in need identified above.

Leaders Are Readers

FIRST IN THE SERIES OF THREE STUDIES:
LEADERSHIP IS DEVELOPED IN OUR WALK

LEADERSHIP TRAIT UNDER CONSTRUCTION: LOVE

• •

WARM-UP: AS CHUCK AND DARRYL WALKED BACK TO THE OFFICE FROM A COFFEE BREAK, CHUCK SAID, "YOU SHOULD READ THE BOOK I JUST FINISHED ON MARKETING IN THE TWENTY-FIRST CENTURY." DARRYL REPLIED, "HOW THICK IS IT?" DISCUSS TOGETHER WHAT "THICKNESS" HAS TO DO WITH IT. MOST OF US TRY TO READ WHEN WE CAN. HAVE EACH ONE IN THE GROUP NAME A BOOK HE READ RECENTLY THAT MADE A DEEP IMPRESSION ON HIM.

BACKGROUND

One of the great leaders of all time served as Israel's king. He was best known as a warrior and military strategist, yet he was also known as a reader. As we begin a series on *Leadership Under Construction,* we do well to examine the life of this man, for he led well, read well, and ended well. Our study today will reveal the first ingredient that qualified his leadership.

(WALK) ⇒

LOVE

READ

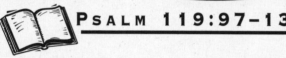
PSALM 119:97–131

QUESTIONS FOR INTERACTION:

❶ What were the real loves of King David, Israel's leader? How was his leadership shaped by these loves?

❷ Why did this king have such a great love for God's Word? How do you think this love came about?

PROMISE KEEPERS®
MEN OF INTEGRITY

3 God's Holy Spirit constructed in King David a deep love for God's Word. If you can, describe how this is beginning to happen in your experience.

4 A certain spiritual leader appears to have a deep love for God's Word, yet a shallow affection for people. Does this bother you? Why?

WRAP-UP:

DISCUSS TOGETHER WHY A LOVE FOR GOD'S WORD MUST BE INCLUDED IN THE CONSTRUCTION OF A SPIRITUAL LEADER.

LET'S PRAY

ONE MINUTE: PRAY SILENTLY ABOUT TODAY'S STUDY
TWO MINUTES: EXPRESS THANKS TO GOD TOGETHER
THREE MINUTES: WRITE IN YOUR PRAYER JOURNAL
FOUR MINUTES: PRAY FOR EACH OTHER

● ●

MY RESPONSE AS A PROMISE KEEPER

1 I will spend ten minutes each workday reading Psalm 119:113–28 as an investment in my spiritual leadership.

2 I will select one book on spiritual leadership (no matter how thick) to read in the coming months.

MONDAY MORNING MUSIC

SECOND IN THE SERIES OF THREE STUDIES:
LEADERSHIP IS DEVELOPED IN OUR WALK

LEADERSHIP TRAIT UNDER CONSTRUCTION: JOY

• •

WARM-UP: DON'T YOU LOVE IT WHEN YOU SEE A MONDAY MORNING COMMUTER MOVING WITH THE MUSIC? DON'T YOU LOVE IT WHEN YOU HEAR YOUR TEENAGER SINGING IN THE SHOWER? DON'T YOU LOVE IT WHEN SOMEONE BEHIND YOU IN THE CHECKOUT LINE WHISTLES A HAPPY TUNE? DISCUSS TOGETHER WHY WE LOVE SUCH MOMENTS. WHAT LIKELY IS TRUE OF THESE PEOPLE WHO HAVE A SONG?

BACKGROUND

The work of rebuilding the wall around Jerusalem was now complete, and they did it in fifty-two days! The workers had not only been required to raise Jerusalem's wall from its ruins with one hand but to wield a sword with the other. The challenge of Nehemiah's leadership had been to direct his people under the worst of construction conditions. Ezra the scribe was instructed to begin reading the book of the law of Moses. As the nation listened, a strange thing happened. In today's study, we will discover Nehemiah's creative alternative to the nation's bleak outlook.

JOY

MEN OF INTEGRITY

READ

NEHEMIAH 8:1–12

QUESTIONS FOR INTERACTION:

1 Why do you suppose Nehemiah, Ezra, and the other spiritual leaders of Israel introduced the reading of the Scriptures as a part of the resettlement of Jerusalem?

2 Why do you think the people wept when they heard the reading of God's Word?

3 Nehemiah recognized the grief of the people he was leading. What do you think he had in mind when he said to them, "The joy of the Lord is your strength" (v. 10)?

4 God's Holy Spirit gives us joy. Why is the joy of the Lord so strengthening in our lives?

WRAP-UP: <u>DISCUSS TOGETHER</u> WHY JOY MUST BE INCLUDED IN THE CONSTRUCTION OF A SPIRITUAL LEADER.

LET'S PRAY: (SEE PRAYER JOURNAL)

• •

MY RESPONSE AS A PROMISE KEEPER

1 I will commit to memory Nehemiah 8:10: "For the joy of the Lord is your strength."

2 If/when I am stuck in Monday morning traffic, I will remind myself that my joy is in the Lord.

BLEAK BLAKE

THIRD IN THE SERIES OF THREE STUDIES:
LEADERSHIP IS DEVELOPED IN OUR WALK

LEADERSHIP TRAIT UNDER CONSTRUCTION: PEACE

● ●

WARM-UP: ANXIETY AND DEPRESSION SEEM TO BE ENDEMIC THESE DAYS. BLEAK BLAKE HAS SPENT NEARLY $300 ALREADY THIS YEAR ON OVER-THE-COUNTER DRUGS TO CALM HIS FEARS AND QUIET HIS HEART. DISCUSS TOGETHER WHY YOU THINK PEACE IS BECOMING SO RARE AMONG SO MANY PEOPLE IN OUR CULTURE.

BACKGROUND

The prophet Isaiah has been appointed leader of a disoriented nation made up of disobedient people. What an assignment! His leadership challenge was both to call the people back to righteous living and to warn them of impending judgment if they didn't heed his call. In today's session, we will discover a leadership trait in Isaiah—something that is easily overlooked, yet essential for directing people.

READ

ISAIAH 26:1–12

QUESTIONS FOR INTERACTION:

❶ There will be a day when the nation of Israel will again be singing. What does their song tell us is their source of national confidence and peace (vv. 1–2)?

❷ Where do we usually look to find peace?

PEACE

3 According to Isaiah, what are some of the benefits of trusting the Lord for His peace?

4 Why do some people never seem to grasp God's peace?

 WRAP-UP: DISCUSS TOGETHER WHY PEACE MUST BE INCLUDED IN THE CONSTRUCTION OF A SPIRITUAL LEADER.

LET'S PRAY: (SEE PRAYER JOURNAL)

MY RESPONSE AS A PROMISE KEEPER

1 There will be moments when I'll need God's peace. I will look to the Holy Spirit to release His peace through me.

2 I will take the leadership challenge of being a peacemaker at work and at home.

CRUSH HOUR

FIRST IN THE SERIES OF THREE STUDIES:
LEADERSHIP IS EXAMINED IN OUR WORK

LEADERSHIP TRAIT UNDER CONSTRUCTION: PATIENCE

• •

WARM-UP:

WE ALL KNOW THAT SITTING IN RUSH-HOUR TRAFFIC TESTS OUR PATIENCE. HOWEVER, THE TEST USUALLY EXTENDS INTO OUR WORKDAY AND OFTEN ALL THE WAY BACK HOME. IMPATIENCE DOES STRANGE THINGS TO US. DISCUSS TOGETHER WHAT YOU HAVE DISCOVERED THAT IMPATIENCE DOES TO YOU.

BACKGROUND

Patience is not a pop-up virtue, but rather a part of the cluster of graces from the Holy Spirit. Webster's dictionary defines *patience* as "bearing pains or trials calmly or without complaint." Maybe we can get a better grasp of this elusive virtue by spending a day with Jesus. We will find Him to be an amazing demonstration of a patient leader.

READ

MARK 5:21–43

QUESTIONS FOR INTERACTION:

1 If you were with Jesus in the "crush hours" of the day just described, what might you have seen challenging His patience?

2 Describe what this day could have been for Jesus had He been impatient.

WALK ⇒ WORK

PATIENCE

❸ What do you learn about patience from watching Jesus on this busy day?

❹ What do you know about Jesus' life that would give Him patience in the crush of the crowd?

WRAP-UP: DISCUSS TOGETHER WHY PATIENCE MUST BE INCLUDED IN THE CONSTRUCTION OF A SPIRITUAL LEADER.

LET'S PRAY: (SEE PRAYER JOURNAL)

MY RESPONSE AS A PROMISE KEEPER

❶ There will be moments when I'll need patience. I will look to the Holy Spirit to release His patience through me.

❷ I will take the leadership challenge and demonstrate patience the next time I am in a pressured situation (likely within the hour).

KILL 'EM WITH KINDNESS

SECOND IN THE SERIES OF THREE STUDIES:
LEADERSHIP IS EXAMINED IN OUR WORK

LEADERSHIP TRAIT UNDER CONSTRUCTION: KINDNESS

WARM-UP: ON THIS PARTICULAR LATE AFTERNOON AFTER WORK, KEITH WAS REALLY IN A HURRY TO GET HOME. IT WAS HIS DAUGHTER'S BIRTHDAY, AND KEITH DID NOT WANT TO MISS A MINUTE OF IT AS HE DID LAST YEAR. RACING DOWN HIGHWAY 36, HE GLANCED IN HIS REARVIEW MIRROR ONLY TO SEE THE FLASHING LIGHTS THAT ARE EVERY SPEEDING DRIVER'S NIGHTMARE. "OH, I HOPE . . . ." TALK TOGETHER ABOUT WHAT KEITH MIGHT HAVE BEEN HOPING FOR IN THIS OFFICER.

BACKGROUND

Leaders who are kind may not come to mind as quickly as those who are remembered for their unkind actions. A workplace leader, filled with the Holy Spirit, will be characterized by an unusual kindness. The woman we will meet in today's study is touched by unusual kindness. Although the story may be familiar, let's take another look at the leader who gave new life to her by His kindness.

READ

JOHN 8:1–11

QUESTIONS FOR INTERACTION:

❶ Why do you think the trapped woman likely knew little about kindness from men around her?

❷ What kindness did Jesus express to the woman? Why do you think He treated her this way?

KINDNESS

PROMISE KEEPERS®
MEN OF INTEGRITY

48

❸ What did kindness do to the woman?

❹ Why do you suppose some leaders in the workplace are hesitant to express kindness?

WRAP-UP: KINDNESS IS IN THE LIST OF QUALITIES THE HOLY SPIRIT PRODUCES WITHIN US WHEN HE FILLS OUR LIVES. DISCUSS TOGETHER WHY KINDNESS MUST BE INCLUDED IN THE CONSTRUCTION OF A SPIRITUAL LEADER.

LET'S PRAY: (SEE PRAYER JOURNAL)

· ·

MY RESPONSE AS A PROMISE KEEPER

❶ There will be moments when I will need to give kindness. I will look to the Holy Spirit to release His kindness through me.

❷ I will take the leadership challenge by expressing kindness to a coworker who especially needs it today.

BEYOND THE CALL OF DUTY

THIRD IN THE SERIES OF THREE STUDIES:
LEADERSHIP IS EXAMINED IN OUR <u>WORK</u>

LEADERSHIP TRAIT UNDER CONSTRUCTION: <u>GOODNESS</u>

• •

WARM-UP: PICTURE A HUNGRY LITTLE BOY IN A WAR-TORN CITY, LOOKING IN THE WINDOW OUTSIDE A BAKERY. A HURRIED SOLDIER OF THE OCCUPYING FORCES, WHILE HURRYING DOWN THE STREET, NEARLY STEPS ON THE LITTLE GUY. <u>DISCUSS TOGETHER</u> WHAT THE SOLDIER MIGHT DO IF HE WERE TO ACT BEYOND THE CALL OF DUTY.

BACKGROUND

Goodness in a leader's life, like kindness, may strike us as not quite fitting. No matter how we may define goodness in the life of a leader, we surely recognize it when we see it. Jesus called His followers to duty when He said, "Let your light shine before men, that they may see your *good* deeds and praise your Father in heaven" (Matt. 5:16, emphasis added). In today's study, we find Jesus' goodness on display in a place where no one else seemed to care.

READ

JOHN 5:1–9

QUESTIONS FOR INTERACTION:

1 Discuss what it must have been like at the pool of Bethesda.

2 As Jesus looked around the pool, why do you suppose He picked out this man to display His goodness?

GOODNESS

3 What did goodness look like to this man, who had been an invalid for so long? Why might it have taken so long to meet a good person?

HARD HAT AREA:

"YOU CANNOT LIVE A PERFECT DAY WITHOUT DOING SOMETHING FOR SOMEONE WHO WILL NEVER BE ABLE TO REPAY YOU."

JOHN WOODEN

4 What might goodness look like in the workplace? Why are workplace leaders hesitant to express goodness?

WRAP-UP: THE APOSTLE PAUL WRITES, "FOR WE ARE GOD'S WORKMANSHIP, CREATED IN CHRIST JESUS TO DO <u>GOOD</u> WORKS, WHICH GOD PREPARED IN ADVANCE FOR US TO DO" (EPH. 2:10, EMPHASIS ADDED). <u>DISCUSS TOGETHER</u> WHAT GOOD WORKS GOD MIGHT BE PREPARING FOR THIS GROUP TO DO . . . BEYOND THE CALL OF DUTY.

LET'S PRAY: (SEE PRAYER JOURNAL)

● ●

MY RESPONSE AS A PROMISE KEEPER

❶ There will be moments when I will need to express goodness. I will look to the Holy Spirit to release His goodness through me.

❷ I will take the leadership challenge of expressing goodness to _____.

SEMPER FI

FIRST IN THE SERIES OF THREE STUDIES:
LEADERSHIP IS TESTED IN OUR **RELATIONSHIPS**

LEADERSHIP TRAIT UNDER CONSTRUCTION: **FAITHFULNESS**

● ●

WARM-UP:

WHO IN THE GROUP RECOGNIZES WHERE TODAY'S SESSION TITLE COMES FROM? IN THE EVENT THAT NO ONE IN THE GROUP IS AN EX-MARINE, SEMPER FI IS A DISTINGUISHING MARK OF A FEW GOOD MEN—ALWAYS FAITHFUL. DISCUSS TOGETHER WHY THE UNITED STATES MARINES WANT THE HEARTBEAT OF THEIR LEADERSHIP TO BE MARKED BY LOYALTY AND FAITHFULNESS.

BACKGROUND

"The word for 'faithfulness' is usually translated 'faith.' But here it seems to mean the faith which invites others to rely on us. More simply, it is not trust but trustworthiness."[1] In today's session, we will meet a man who was given great leadership opportunity but was self-detoured for years in order that he might learn faithfulness.

1. J. R. STOTT, BAPTISM AND FULLNESS (DOWNER'S GROVE, IL: INTERVARSITY PRESS, 1976), 77.

READ

ACTS 12:24–13:15; 15:36–41

QUESTIONS FOR INTERACTION:

1 What was the sharp disagreement between Paul and Barnabas? Why do you think Barnabas was able to overlook John Mark's earlier defection, whereas Paul could not?

2 The fact that John Mark was chosen to travel with the apostles meant that he likely met some high qualifications. How could he have fooled his companions?

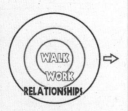

WALK
WORK
RELATIONSHIPS
⇒

FAITHFULNESS

❸ Later on in John Mark's life story, he would become highly regarded by the apostle Paul (see Col. 4:10 and 2 Tim. 4:11). How might we explain the transformation?

❹ What value do you place on faithfulness? Why? How might faithfulness be demonstrated in the workplace?

WRAP-UP: DISCUSS TOGETHER WHY YOU THINK FAITHFULNESS IS INCLUDED IN THE LIST OF THE FRUIT OF THE HOLY SPIRIT AND THEREFORE IN THE CONSTRUCTION OF A SPIRITUAL LEADER.

LET'S PRAY: (SEE PRAYER JOURNAL)

● ●

MY RESPONSE AS A PROMISE KEEPER

❶ There will be opportunities in my workplace when my faithfulness will be tested. I will look to the Holy Spirit to release His faithfulness through me.

❷ I will take the leadership challenge and demonstrate faithfulness as a value in my workplace by _____.

GENTLE BEN

. . . .

WARM-UP:

A MAJOR AIRLINE IS FACING A CRIPPLING STRIKE. THE MECHANICS FEEL CHEATED IN THEIR WAGES. THE PILOTS UNION IS SYMPATHETIC WITH THE MECHANICS' ISSUES. YOU ARE PART OF THE MANAGEMENT TEAM RESPONSIBLE TO RESOLVE THE ALREADY-EXPLOSIVE BATTLE BETWEEN LABOR AND MANAGEMENT. THIS MORNING, LOOKING FOR COUNSEL IN YOUR DAILY BIBLE READING, YOU DISCOVERED GENTLENESS TO BE ONE OF THE MARKS OF A GODLY LEADER. DISCUSS TOGETHER HOW GENTLENESS MIGHT FIND ITS WAY INTO YOUR STRATEGY FOR RESOLUTION.

BACKGROUND

A gentle leader in the workplace seems like an oxymoron—the two just don't go together. However, Paul's use of the word tells a different story. In today's session, we will discover the apostle listing a number of qualities needed for dealing with agitating people. He suggests a picture of a leader who can act decisively yet express gentleness.

READ

2 TIMOTHY 2:23–3:5

QUESTIONS FOR INTERACTION:

❶ Why do you think Paul says that we must steer clear of argumentative discussions?

❷ When we must be involved with agitated people in our workplace, what can we learn to do from what the apostle tells us?

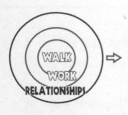

WALK
WORK
RELATIONSHIPS ⇨

GENTLENESS

3 When God is working through the gentle leader, what does He hope to do?

4 There may be times in our workplaces when expressing gentleness is impossible. From both the passage and your experience, when might this be?

WRAP-UP: GENTLENESS IS LISTED AMONG THE FRUIT OF THE HOLY SPIRIT AND THEREFORE MUST BE INCLUDED IN THE CONSTRUCTION OF A SPIRITUAL LEADER. DISCUSS TOGETHER WHAT MIGHT HAPPEN IF YOU RESPONDED WITH GENTLENESS TO A CONFUSED TEENAGER AT HOME.

 LET'S PRAY: (SEE PRAYER JOURNAL)

• •

MY RESPONSE AS A PROMISE KEEPER

1 There will be opportunities in my workplace when my gentleness will be tested. I will look to the Holy Spirit to release His gentleness through me.

2 I will take the leadership challenge by responding with gentleness tonight to someone in my home.

ROCK SLIDE

LEADERSHIP TRAIT UNDER CONSTRUCTION: SELF-CONTROL

• •

WARM-UP:

MIKE IS KNOWN AROUND TOWN AS "THE ROCK." HE IS A PICTURE OF SELF-CONTROL AND TIGHT-GUT TOUGHNESS IN ALL HE DOES. IN OTHER WORDS, HE'S DISCIPLINED TO THE MAX. HOWEVER, THE OTHER SIDE OF THIS MOUNTAIN-MAN IS LOOSE SHALE, A SIDE OF MIKE NOBODY REALLY KNOWS. RECENTLY MIKE HAS CONFESSED TO YOU THAT HE IS WEAK AND VULNERABLE WHEN IT COMES TO HIS SECRET DESIRES FOR WOMEN. DISCUSS TOGETHER WHAT MIGHT BE SOME REASONS THAT HIS SELF-CONTROL SEEMS TO FALL APART IN THIS AREA.

BACKGROUND

Times have obviously changed since the apostle Paul wrote this letter. However, our common human condition has not changed. The need for control over our lives remains constant. In particular, the area of sexual morals needs a focus of self-control. In our session today, we will be instructed as to how to please God and prevent a moral rock slide.

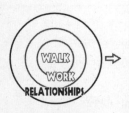

SELF-CONTROL

READ

1 THESSALONIANS 4:1-8

QUESTIONS FOR INTERACTION:

1 Paul is writing to a church. Why might even these people need a call to sexual purity?

2 Why should God be so concerned that we exercise sexual self-control? What has He done to help us?

3 In this section, the apostle describes the rock slide of immorality of the person who doesn't know God. Where have you seen this slide typically beginning and ending?

4 A lack of self-control in the sexual area has severe implications. Why?

 WRAP-UP. IN LIGHT OF TODAY'S DISCUSSION, <u>TALK TOGETHER</u> ABOUT WHY YOU ARE THANKFUL THAT SELF-CONTROL IS INCLUDED IN THE FRUIT OF THE SPIRIT.

LET'S PRAY: (SEE PRAYER JOURNAL)

MY RESPONSE AS A PROMISE KEEPER

1 There will be opportunities in my workplace when my self-control will be tested. I will look to the Holy Spirit to release His self-control through me.

2 I will take the leadership challenge of exercising self-control in the area of

_____.

SCRATCH AND SNIFF

FIRST IN THE SERIES OF THREE STUDIES:
LEADERSHIP IS EXPRESSED IN OUR MINISTRY

LEADERSHIP TRAIT UNDER CONSTRUCTION: THINKS CLEARLY

• •

WARM-UP: HAVE EACH PERSON IN THE GROUP TAKE A PIECE OF PAPER AND LIST FIVE OR SIX THINGS THAT REALLY MATTER TO HIM. THIS LIST MIGHT INCLUDE SUCH TANGIBLE THINGS AS THE NAMES OF PEOPLE OR A HOME. IT MAY INCLUDE SUCH INTANGIBLE THINGS AS A DREAM OR YOUR REPUTATION. NOW, TALK ABOUT WHAT IS ON THE LISTS.

BACKGROUND

READ

Down through the centuries, leaders have come and gone. Each hoped he or she would make lasting contributions to humanity. Among the unique contributions of Jesus Christ was His modeling of three leadership qualities: thinking clearly, feeling deeply, and acting consistently. In today's study, we will find Jesus helping a young man who was too distracted by his wealth to think clearly.

MARK 10:17–27

QUESTIONS FOR INTERACTION:

1 What do you think prompted this man's question when he first came to Jesus?

2 How did the clear thinking of Jesus challenge the rich man's thinking?

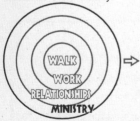

THINKS CLEARLY

PROMISE
KEEPERS®
MEN OF INTEGRITY

58

3 It is interesting that Jesus only quoted the last six of the Ten Commandments. Why do you think He did this for this rich young man?

4 As Jesus' clear thinking made its impact on this man, what did He ask him to do and why?

WRAP-UP.

LOOKING BACK TO THE LISTS YOU MADE IN TODAY'S WARM-UP, SCRATCH OUT:
- ANYTHING THAT CAN BURN (EXCEPT PEOPLE, OF COURSE);
- ANYTHING TAKEN AWAY WITH LOSS OF HEALTH (SHORT OF DEATH);
- ANYTHING ELIMINATED WITH A SUDDEN DOWNTURN IN THE ECONOMY.

TALK TOGETHER ABOUT WHAT IS LEFT ON YOUR LISTS.

 LET'S PRAY: (SEE PRAYER JOURNAL)

• •

MY RESPONSE AS A PROMISE KEEPER

❶ I will think clearly about what really matters from my list discussed in today's Wrap-Up.

❷ There may be an opportunity to interact with a person like we met in today's study. I will take the opportunity to help this person to think clearly about his

_____.

TEMPLE TANTRUM?

SECOND IN THE SERIES OF THREE STUDIES:
LEADERSHIP IS EXPRESSED IN OUR MINISTRY

LEADERSHIP TRAIT UNDER CONSTRUCTION: FEELS DEEPLY

• •

WARM-UP:

BANKS TRAIN THEIR BRANCH MANAGERS NOT ONLY TO LEAD PROFITABLE OPERATIONS, BUT ALSO TO ENSURE EXCELLENT CUSTOMER RELATIONS. WHEN BILL, FIRST FRIENDLY'S BANK MANAGER, WAS REVIEWING THE DAY'S ACTIVITIES, HE NOTED AN UNUSUALLY LARGE WITHDRAWAL OF FUNDS. UPON INVESTIGATION, HE LEARNED THAT A PARTICULAR BANK CUSTOMER THAT DAY CAME BY TO DO BUSINESS WITH FIRST FRIENDLY'S LEAD LOAN OFFICER. A RECEPTIONIST INFORMED HIM THAT THE OFFICER WAS AWAY. UPON LEAVING, THE CUSTOMER ASKED TO HAVE HIS PARKING COUPON VALIDATED. THE RECEPTIONIST SAID SHE WAS UNABLE TO DO SO SINCE HE HADN'T DONE ANY BUSINESS AT THE BANK. "OKAY, MA'AM, THEN I WILL DO SOME BUSINESS HERE!" WITH THAT HE INSTRUCTED HER TO TRANSFER ALL HIS FUNDS, $90,000, TO THE BANK ACROSS THE STREET. AS THE BANK'S LEADER, BILL MUST THINK CLEARLY, FEEL DEEPLY, AND ACT CONSISTENTLY. DISCUSS TOGETHER WHAT THAT WILL MEAN FOR HIM.

BACKGROUND

Does the Scripture for today's session suggest that Jesus was out of control, having a tantrum? Was His normally clear thinking being fogged by what He was feeling? Does Jesus keep these in balance?

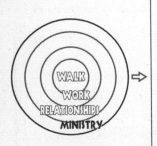

FEELS DEEPLY

READ

MARK 11:11, 15–19

QUESTIONS FOR INTERACTION:

1 It certainly seems out of character for Jesus to react this way. What do you suppose He was thinking this day in Jerusalem?

2 Obviously, Jesus was feeling deeply about what He saw in the temple. Was He overreacting? Why/Why not?

3 Jesus was thinking clearly and feeling deeply in this frustrating situation. Why do you suppose He used such extreme measures?

4 Talk about a time when you either participated in or observed someone in leadership reacting strongly (appropriately so) in a frustrating situation.

WRAP-UP. AS PROMISE BUILDERS IN THE MARKETPLACE, TOGETHER PICK ONE ISSUE (E.G., FAIR LABOR PRACTICES, ETHICAL MATTERS, DISCRIMINATION) THAT SHOULD GRIP US TO TAKE STEPS OF ACTION MUCH AS JESUS DID.

LET'S PRAY: (SEE PRAYER JOURNAL)

• •

MY RESPONSE AS A PROMISE KEEPER

❶ I must not live emotionally detached from the issues in my workplace, but rather I will feel deeply about them.

❷ To begin feeling deeply about my coworkers, I will pray for two of them by name each day this week: _____.

CALIFORNIA DREAMIN'

THIRD IN THE SERIES OF THREE STUDIES:
LEADERSHIP IS EXPRESSED IN OUR MINISTRY

LEADERSHIP TRAIT UNDER CONSTRUCTION: ACTS CONSISTENTLY

• •

WARM-UP: RICK IS A SENIOR IN A SACRAMENTO HIGH SCHOOL. HIS BASKETBALL TEAM WAS LEAGUE CHAMPIONS LAST YEAR AND CINCHED THE TITLE AGAIN THIS YEAR. RICK IS BEING STRONGLY RECRUITED BY THE HEAD COACH AT THE UNIVERSITY OF MASSACHUSETTS. HOWEVER, RICK HAS BEEN DREAMING ALL HIS LIFE ABOUT PLAYING COLLEGE BALL CLOSE TO HOME. TALK TOGETHER ABOUT WHAT WILL BE DIFFICULT FOR RICK WITH THIS CHALLENGE TO LEAVE CALIFORNIA AND PLAY AT THE UNIVERSITY OF MASSACHUSETTS.

BACKGROUND

In Jesus' strategy of building the kingdom of God, He was selecting His core of future leaders. They would later be called the apostles, men who would set the course doctrinally and strategically for the church. He must have seen in these common men the ability to think clearly, feel deeply, and act consistently.

READ

MARK 1:14–20

QUESTIONS FOR INTERACTION:

1 Jesus was more than an itinerant preacher and miracle worker. He was a strategist. From what Mark tells us in this section, how do we know Jesus was a strategist?

2 These clear-thinking businessmen must have felt they were acting consistently when they left everything to follow Jesus. What must have been so persuasive about His call?

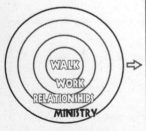

ACTS CONSISTENTLY

PROMISE
KEEPERS®
MEN OF INTEGRITY

3 About what must Jesus have been feeling so deeply that He would ask these men to abandon everything?

4 Agree/Disagree: Answering the call to follow Jesus always involves reaching people for Him. Why/Why not?

WRAP-UP: THE CALL OF JESUS TO YOU MAY NOT MEAN THAT YOU WILL LEAVE YOUR WORKPLACE. HOWEVER, HE HAS CALLED YOU. IF YOU ARE TO ACT CONSISTENTLY WITH HIS CALL TO BE "FISHERS OF MEN" (V. 17), <u>DISCUSS TOGETHER</u> HOW THIS WILL AFFECT THE WAY YOU SEE AND THINK ABOUT YOUR WORKPLACE.

 LET'S PRAY: (SEE PRAYER JOURNAL)

MY RESPONSE AS A PROMISE KEEPER

1 Since I have been called as a "fisher of men," I will anticipate that the Lord will give me opportunities for doing this wherever I go.

2 I will take an hour within this coming week to reflect on the twelve leadership traits of this series. I will pray to be this kind of leader.

SERMON ON THE AMOUNT

FIRST IN THE SERIES OF THREE STUDIES: FINANCIAL
PERSPECTIVE IS DEVELOPED IN OUR <u>WALK</u>

FINANCIAL ISSUE UNDER CONSTRUCTION: <u>PERSPECTIVE</u>

• •

WARM-UP: DON AND HIS WIFE AGREED TO MEET AT THE SOUTH EXIT OF THEIR
COMMUNITY'S NEWLY OPENED MALL. ARRIVING ABOUT TWENTY MINUTES
EARLY, HE HAD TIME TO OBSERVE HOW MANY SHOPPERS WERE TAKING
ADVANTAGE OF THE GRAND-OPENING SALES. AS A CHRISTIAN, DON
WONDERED WHAT DIFFERENCES THERE SHOULD BE BETWEEN CHRISTIANS
AND NON-CHRISTIANS WHEN IT COMES TO SPENDING MONEY AND
GATHERING POSSESSIONS. <u>DISCUSS TOGETHER</u> HOW YOU MIGHT ANSWER
THAT QUESTION.

BACKGROUND

This is the first of twelve
sessions dealing with
finances. Our starting
point is to get perspective.
The world around us has
delivered a message that
says basic needs are met
with money. Jesus, in His
Sermon on the Mount,
cuts right across our
contemporary perspective.
He teaches in today's
session that possessions
are to be held lightly,
resulting in worry-free
living.

READ

MATTHEW 6:19–34

QUESTIONS FOR INTERACTION:

❶ What comes to mind when you think of "wealth"? What
would you consider to be some of wealth's benefits?

❷ Why is Jesus so concerned that we make good investments
of our treasures?

PERSPECTIVE

PROMISE
KEEPERS®
MEN OF INTEGRITY

❸ The world of business is driven by making a profit. How does a Christian businessperson work within this framework and yet serve God?

❹ Jesus identified the common needs of the people of His day. What is the disadvantage of having enough money to supply all these needs?

WRAP-UP:

IF WE WERE TO FOLLOW JESUS' CALL TO "SEEK FIRST HIS KINGDOM AND HIS RIGHTEOUSNESS" (v. 33), TALK TOGETHER OF WHAT WE MIGHT BE DOING. MAKE YOUR SUGGESTIONS PRACTICAL.

LET'S PRAY

ONE MINUTE: PRAY SILENTLY ABOUT TODAY'S STUDY
TWO MINUTES: EXPRESS THANKS TO GOD TOGETHER
THREE MINUTES: WRITE IN YOUR PRAYER JOURNAL
FOUR MINUTES: PRAY FOR EACH OTHER

MY RESPONSE AS A PROMISE KEEPER

❶ I will take inventory of my heart by noting where my "treasures" are.

❷ I will recognize that I can serve God in my workplace while helping the company profit.

TWISTER

• •

WARM-UP:

LIFE IN "TORNADO ALLEY" IS JUST DOWNRIGHT SCARY. YOU NEVER KNOW WHAT A HOT SUMMER DAY MIGHT BRING. AS AN INSURANCE AGENT, YOUR CONVERSATION WITH THE HARGRAVES THIS AFTERNOON IS GOING TO BE MORE THAN AN ASSESSMENT OF DAMAGE; YOU KNOW THEY HAVE LOST EVERYTHING. TALK TOGETHER OF WHAT YOU MIGHT SAY TO SOMEONE WHO HAS LOST IT ALL TO A TWISTER.

BACKGROUND

Today's section for study is a parable about the kingdom of heaven. Jesus tells what it would be like if His kingdom were on earth and He were its Master. Although this has not yet happened, the money management principles are applicable for those of us who now give Him His rightful ownership over our life and possessions.

READ

MATTHEW 25:14–30

QUESTIONS FOR INTERACTION:

1 Ownership has its privileges. What were those privileges to the master in this story?

2 What do you suppose the master was thinking when he gave differing amounts of money to each of the money managers?

3 What do you suppose the three money managers were thinking when they were given differing amounts of the master's money? Note: A talent was worth more than fifteen years' wages of a laborer.

MONEY MANAGEMENT

PROMISE
K E E P E R S®
MEN OF INTEGRITY

④ Given the resources, what were the temptations these money managers likely faced? What would have restrained them?

⑤ Some might think that the master was overly severe with the one-talent worker. What does the owner's reaction tell us?

WRAP-UP: THE OWNER HAS GIVEN EACH OF US MONEY AND POSSESSIONS TO MANAGE. HAVE <u>EACH PERSON TELL ABOUT</u> ONE THING HE HAS LEARNED ABOUT MANAGING WHAT GOD HAS ENTRUSTED TO HIM.

 LET'S PRAY: (SEE PRAYER JOURNAL)

MY RESPONSE AS A PROMISE KEEPER

❶ I will pause to ask the Owner for wisdom each time I open my checkbook.

❷ I will identify and pray about one area that needs to change in my management of what He has entrusted to me.

CONTENTED IN COLORADO?

THIRD IN THE SERIES OF THREE STUDIES: FINANCIAL
PERSPECTIVE IS DEVELOPED IN OUR <u>WALK</u>

FINANCIAL ISSUE UNDER CONSTRUCTION: <u>CONTENTMENT</u>

• •

WARM-UP: PEOPLE OFTEN MOVE TO DIFFERENT PARTS OF THE COUNTRY FOR
DISCOVERY OF BETTER JOBS, SCHOOLS, CLIMATE . . . LIFE. FROZEN
MINNESOTANS SCURRY TO SUNNY ARIZONA; CROWDED CALIFORNIANS
MIGRATE TO A QUIETER COLORADO. <u>DISCUSS TOGETHER</u>: IF YOU HAVE TO
MOVE SIX INCHES FROM WHERE YOU ARE RIGHT NOW IN ORDER TO BE
HAPPY, WILL YOU EVER BE REALLY HAPPY?

BACKGROUND

The apostle Paul is
writing a letter to his
Philippian friends from a
prison cell in Rome. By
this time he has walked
with Jesus Christ for
about half of his life, thirty
years or so. Although he
has been entertained in
kings' courts, he has paid
a price for following
Jesus. Wisdom comes
with time and experience.
This prisoner has much to
tell us about contentment
in today's session.

(WALK) ⇨

CONTENTMENT

PROMISE
K E E P E R S ®
MEN OF INTEGRITY

READ

PHILIPPIANS
4:10–20

QUESTIONS FOR INTERACTION:

❶ Why do you think it is difficult to experience contentment
in the American culture?

❷ Word is out in the Roman prison that the captured Paul of
Tarsus is strangely at peace these days in his cell.
Cellmates and guards alike want to know why. How do
you suppose Paul is answering that question?

3 Apparently contentment is a virtue to be learned, according to this prisoner. What keeps us from experiencing contentment as Paul did?

4 If being well-fed, having plenty, and never being in need describes our lives, what does the contented prisoner Paul say we will miss?

WRAP-UP: LET'S PAINT A NEW PICTURE OF OURSELVES AND COLOR IT WITH CONTENTMENT. <u>TALK TOGETHER</u> OF WHAT IT WOULD LOOK LIKE.

LET'S PRAY: (SEE PRAYER JOURNAL)

• •

MY RESPONSE AS A PROMISE KEEPER

❶ I will give thanks every day this week for all I've been given.

❷ Whenever I feel the need for contentment, I will repeat the words of Philippians 4:13: "I can do everything through him who gives me strength."

TREADMILL TO NOWHERE

FIRST IN THE SERIES OF THREE STUDIES: FINANCIAL
PERFORMANCE IS EXAMINED IN OUR WORK

FINANCIAL ISSUE UNDER CONSTRUCTION: SECURITY

● ●

WARM-UP:

TODD HAS AVERAGED SEVENTY HOURS PER WEEK IN HIS JOB FOR THE LAST
SIX MONTHS. HE CONSOLES HIS WIFE AND FAMILY THAT THESE LONG HOURS
ARE ONLY TEMPORARY. "IT WON'T BE LONG, LINDA, AND WE WILL HAVE
ENOUGH MONEY TO BEGIN ENJOYING LIFE. I'M EAGER TO TAKE US ON THAT
LONG-AWAITED VACATION WE'VE DREAMED OF, IN THAT FORD EXPLORER WE
WILL NOW BE ABLE TO AFFORD." TALK TOGETHER OF HOW OUR TREADMILL
CULTURE IS DEFINING "FINANCIAL SECURITY."

BACKGROUND

There is a group
of people in our
churches who are likely
misunderstood—we think
they have no needs. They
are the men and women
who are apparently
financially secure. Paul
the apostle simply calls
them "the rich." But they
have great needs
because their money
could be keeping them
from experiencing the
quality of life only God
can give. In today's study,
we will discover God's will
for the financially secure.

SECURITY

MEN OF INTEGRITY

READ

1 TIMOTHY 6:11–21
(FOCUS ON 6:17–19)

QUESTIONS FOR INTERACTION:

1 The apostle Paul is instructing young Timothy to warn
people who are financially secure in his church of a false
hope of economic security. Why does he give this warning?

2 Why does Paul say we are to set our hopes for a secure
future on God? What have you learned about this?

3 If we should become financially secure, what activities does Paul call us to do? Give some examples of people you know of who are doing this (e.g., former President Jimmy Carter and Habitat for Humanity).

4 When we transfer our hopes for a secure future from money to the Lord, the apostle Paul promises we will "take hold of the life that is truly life" (v. 19). Explore what this promise could mean.

WRAP-UP: IN LIGHT OF TODAY'S STUDY, GO BACK TO TODD AND LINDA IN THE WARM-UP. TOGETHER, DECIDE WHAT WOULD BE GOOD COUNSEL TO THIS YOUNG COUPLE ON THEIR TREADMILL TO NOWHERE.

 LET'S PRAY: (SEE PRAYER JOURNAL)

MY RESPONSE AS A PROMISE KEEPER

1 I will be alert to observe how God is providing for me, even in the smallest ways.

2 I will consider how to use my financial means more generously.

An Honest Day's Work

• •

WARM-UP:

ON HIS WAY TO WORK, JIM IS AGAIN CONFRONTED WITH THE SAME HOMELESS PERSON PLEADING FROM HER CARDBOARD SIGN, "PLEASE GIVE ME A SMALL GIFT TO HELP PROVIDE FOR MY FAMILY!" JIM WONDERS WHETHER OR NOT HE SHOULD. HE DOESN'T. LATER THAT MORNING, OUTSIDE HIS OFFICE BUILDING ON A FRESH AIR BREAK, HE SAYS TO HIS COLLEAGUES, "WHY DO I FEEL GUILTY ABOUT IGNORING THESE HOMELESS PEOPLE?" TALK TOGETHER OF WHAT YOU MIGHT ADD TO THE CONVERSATION.

BACKGROUND

The Bible is more than just the Holy Book of our religion: It communicates God's will for our everyday lives. Work is a major part of every day, and from this work we hope to make money. Today we will look into two sections of Scripture and discover two uses of our money that will give new meaning to our work.

READ

EPHESIANS 4:28; 1 TIMOTHY 5:1–8

QUESTIONS FOR INTERACTION:

1 What are some of the reasons people steal? Why do you think the apostle contrasted an honest day's work with stealing?

2 Paul suggests a reason to work that may be radical, according to our culture. What is it?

MEANING FROM WORK

❸ Why do you think Paul speaks in such severe terms regarding the one who doesn't provide for his family?

❹ One fundamental principle of Christianity is working so that we can care for others and provide for our families. Why are absent fathers and mothers so common in our world?

WRAP-UP: THE MEANING MOST PEOPLE ASSIGN TO THEIR JOBS IS SIMPLY TO PAY THEIR BILLS. HOWEVER, TODAY WE HAVE DISCOVERED TWO PURPOSES FOR WORK THAT GIVE NEW MEANING TO IT. SUMMARIZE WHAT THESE ARE, AND <u>TALK TOGETHER ABOUT</u> HOW THIS MAY CHANGE THE WAY YOU THINK OF YOUR WORK LIFE.

 LET'S PRAY: (SEE PRAYER JOURNAL)

• •

MY RESPONSE AS A PROMISE KEEPER

❶ I will be available to give a portion of what I earn to someone I know who has a financial need.

❷ As a family, we will discuss together how we are doing in providing for our needs.

YOU CAN TRUST ME

• •

WARM-UP:

JIM OWNS A SMALL BUSINESS. HE APPRECIATES THE DEPENDABILITY OF HIS EMPLOYEES. IN PARTICULAR JIM IS GRATEFUL FOR HIS CONTROLLER, TOM, WHO IS A "YOU CAN TRUST ME" KIND OF OFFICER. LAST WEEK JIM RECEIVED A LETTER FROM THE IRS CHALLENGING HIS COMPANY'S EXPENSE ACCOUNTS. A SMILE CROSSED HIS LIPS, KNOWING THAT TOM WOULD BE READY TO REFUTE WHATEVER ALLEGATIONS WERE BROUGHT AGAINST HIS COMPANY'S FINANCES. <u>DISCUSS TOGETHER</u> WHY CORPORATE LEADERSHIP HAS VERY HIGH STANDARDS FOR ITS FINANCIAL OFFICERS.

BACKGROUND

Bosses and employers alike have a reasonable expectation that their workers be dependable and trustworthy. Whether it's coming to work on time or completing a project according to the plan, diligence is prized by those in authority. Today's section for study is a parable Jesus told to illustrate the importance of diligence and trustworthiness in the workplace.

READ

LUKE 12:35–48

QUESTIONS FOR INTERACTION:

1 What did Jesus say some of the rewards are of being trustworthy servants?

2 How do we explain the actions of the servant to compromise his master's orders in verse 45?

WALK ⇒ WORK

TRUSTWORTHINESS

3 Some fellow workers, thought to be generally trustworthy, prove otherwise when given the responsibility for company finances. Why?

4 The master exercised severe punishment on the untrustworthy servant. What might this punishment look like in today's workplace?

WRAP-UP: HAVE <u>EACH PERSON TELL</u> OF AN AREA IN HIS LIFE WHEREIN "MUCH HAS BEEN GIVEN" (E.G., MAKING MONEY, BUSINESS SAVVY, PEOPLE SKILLS, VISION). HOW ARE YOU TRYING TO DEMONSTRATE TRUSTWORTHINESS IN THAT AREA?

LET'S PRAY: (SEE PRAYER JOURNAL)

MY RESPONSE AS A PROMISE KEEPER

❶ I will be alert to the reality that my trustworthiness is truly a matter of my integrity before the Lord.

❷ I will examine my trustworthiness in the finances entrusted to me. I may need to _____.

PLASTIC SURGERY

FIRST IN THE SERIES OF THREE STUDIES: FINANCIAL PRACTICES ARE TESTED IN OUR <u>RELATIONSHIPS</u>

FINANCIAL ISSUE UNDER CONSTRUCTION: <u>LIFESTYLE</u>

. . . .

WARM-UP:

IT'S FRIDAY EVENING, THE WEEKEND IS HERE, AND DENNIS AND DARLENE HAVE FINISHED A LIGHT SUPPER AT A FAST-FOOD RESTAURANT NEXT TO THE MALL. WALKING THROUGH THE MALL TO GRAB SOME ICE CREAM, THEY PASS ONE OF THE MAJOR DEPARTMENT STORES. IN THE WINDOW, DENNIS SEES A BUSINESS SUIT THAT TRIGGERS THIS CONVERSATION: "HONEY, I NEED THAT SUIT FOR MY PRESENTATION IN NEW YORK NEXT WEEK." DARLENE RESPONDS, "I'M NOT SURE THERE'S ROOM FOR A $400 CHARGE LEFT ON OUR CREDIT CARD." WITH SOME PRODDING BY HER HUSBAND ABOUT THEIR CREDIT CONDITION, SHE EXPLAINS THAT SHE HAD TO GET A DRESS FOR MOTHER'S DAY AND THAT SHE HAD RUN OUT OF MAKEUP. <u>DISCUSS TOGETHER</u>: DO YOU THINK HE GOT THE SUIT? WHY/WHY NOT?

BACKGROUND

At the point we make contact with the world's system of values and beliefs, we risk erosion of God's work in our lives. The apostle John, in characteristic black-and-white style, challenges us to take a closer look at whom and what we love in this world. This challenge might make us consider "plastic surgery" on our credit card spending.

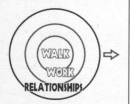

LIFESTYLE

PROMISE KEEPERS®
MEN OF INTEGRITY

READ

1 JOHN 2:15–17

QUESTIONS FOR INTERACTION:

❶ John tells us that the worldly person is driven by three motivators. What are they, and what do they motivate this person to do?

❷ When John says, "If anyone loves the world, the love of the Father is not in him" (v. 15), he is leaving no middle ground. What is at stake here?

3 How do the three motivators John mentions usually cause financial debt?

4 The three motivators John mentions also cause conflicts in relationships. What are some ways you have seen this happen?

WRAP-UP: IF YOU ARE IN DEBT, YOU'RE NOT ALONE. AMERICANS OWE A STAGGERING $1.2 TRILLION ON THEIR CREDIT CARDS. TALK TOGETHER ABOUT HOW WE CAN GET THE UPPER HAND ON CREDIT CARD DEBT.

 LET'S PRAY: (SEE PRAYER JOURNAL)

. . . .

MY RESPONSE AS A PROMISE KEEPER

1 I will make plans to begin to reduce my indebtedness. I must break its power over me, and this may involve plastic surgery.

2 When I am tempted to increase my indebtedness, I will recall God's command to love Him above all things.

DRIVEN

WARM-UP:

DRIVING INTO WORK EARLY THIS MORNING, YOU GLANCE IN YOUR REARVIEW MIRROR. RIGHT ON YOUR BUMPER IS A CLASSY-LOOKING LADY IN A CLASSY-LOOKING LEXUS. AS SHE ZIPS BY, YOU NOTICE SHE'S LOCKED ONTO HER CELL PHONE WITH A TENSE AND HURRIED LOOK ON HER FACE. TALK TOGETHER OF WHAT CHOICES THIS WOMAN HAS LIKELY MADE TO GET WHERE SHE IS.

BACKGROUND

We know from biblical history that Lemuel of Proverbs 31:1 is, in fact, young King Solomon. We see him in today's section of Scripture as he learns what to look for in an excellent wife. One would think that his father, King David, would be his teacher. However, we will discover that his mother is his mentor. God's grace has transformed her life such that she values the disciplines in the description of the excellent wife: Her name is Bathsheba.

GOALS & PLANNING

READ

PROVERBS 31:1-31
(FOCUS ON 31:10-31)

QUESTIONS FOR INTERACTION:

1 What were the benefits to the Proverbs 31 woman from her driven yet poised lifestyle?

2 How did this woman's choices affect her relationships?

3 What might have been some of the financial goals of this diligent wife such that she could "laugh at the days to come" (v. 25)?

4 This outstanding businesswoman apparently had a very supportive mate. What must he have been like?

WRAP-UP: WE ADMIRE THE ACHIEVEMENTS OF THIS WOMAN AND WE DISCOVER IN VERSE 30 THE HEART OF HER SUCCESS. TALK TOGETHER ABOUT HER SECRET. STOP FOR A MINUTE AND HAVE EACH PERSON IDENTIFY AND PRAISE SOMEONE HE KNOWS WHO IS LIKE THIS PERSON.

 LET'S PRAY: (SEE PRAYER JOURNAL)

MY RESPONSE AS A PROMISE KEEPER

1 I will write a first draft of some financial goals for the rest of the year.

2 I will test these goals in my budget and checkbook for one month.

I GAVE AT THE OFFICE

FINANCIAL ISSUE UNDER CONSTRUCTION: BUDGETING

• •

WARM-UP:

LET'S ASSUME FOR A MOMENT THAT YOU ARE A PERSON OF INFLUENCE IN THE FORMATION OF YOUR COMPANY'S BUDGETING OF RESOURCES (E.G., FINANCES, PERSONNEL, SPACE ALLOCATION). A CONSULTANT TO YOUR COMPANY'S PLANNING PROCESS HAS RECOMMENDED THAT YOUR LEADERSHIP ALLOCATE A PERCENTAGE OF YOUR RESOURCES TO CHARITABLE CAUSES. TALK TOGETHER OF SOME EXAMPLES OF CHARITIES THAT MIGHT FULFILL THIS RECOMMENDATION.[1]

BACKGROUND

In ancient biblical times, the centerpieces of a nation's wealth and glory were its places of worship. So, it was of special concern to King David that Israel's temple to the one true God be the masterpiece among the nations. No expense would be spared. We are about to discover how business and personal budgeting contributed to the success of this glorious undertaking.

READ

1 CHRONICLES 29:1–19

QUESTIONS FOR INTERACTION:

1 What motivated King David to allocate resources out of the kingdom budget for the building of the house of God?

2 What benefits came when the king himself began providing generously from his personal budget?

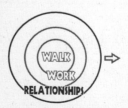

WALK
WORK
RELATIONSHIPS

BUDGETING

PROMISE
KEEPERS®
MEN OF INTEGRITY

1. Recommended resource for budgeting: *Mastering Your Money: Money Management for the Financial Realities of the Nineties*, by Ron Blue.

❸ Had the king not found within his heart and personal budget the resources to give to the temple, how might this grand endeavor have been different?

❹ The ability to give of our resources requires a certain amount of good money management. Budgets are involved. Discuss why you think many people resist the idea of budgeting.

WRAP-UP: HAVE <u>EACH GROUP MEMBER TELL</u> TWO PRINCIPLES HE HAS DISCOVERED IN HIS EXPERIENCE WITH BUDGETING.

 LET'S PRAY: (SEE PRAYER JOURNAL)

• •

MY RESPONSE AS A PROMISE KEEPER

❶ I will pray this prayer daily: "Lord, increase my devotion to You and Your work around me."

❷ I will adjust my budgeting priorities to reflect this devotion.

GIVERS' REMORSE

FIRST IN THE SERIES OF THREE STUDIES: FINANCIAL PROVISIONS ARE EXPRESSED IN OUR MINISTRY

FINANCIAL ISSUE UNDER CONSTRUCTION: PRINCIPLES OF GIVING

● ●

WARM-UP:

WE ALL KNOW ABOUT "BUYERS' REMORSE"—THAT SINKING FEELING OF WISHING WE HADN'T SPENT THE MONEY. "GIVERS' REMORSE" IS SIMILAR—THE SINKING FEELING OF WISHING WE HADN'T GIVEN WITHOUT MORE THOUGHT. JOHN AND CARRIE HAVE JUST RETURNED FROM THEIR FIRST TERM AS MISSIONARIES IN ETHIOPIA. THE CONGREGATION IS DEEPLY MOVED BY THEIR REPORTS OF GREAT RESPONSIVENESS TO THE GOSPEL, ALONG WITH THE GREAT PHYSICAL NEEDS THERE. AT THE CONCLUSION OF THEIR REPORT, THE MISSIONS COMMITTEE CHAIRPERSON CHALLENGES THE CONGREGATION TO GIVE GENEROUSLY TO THIS FINE COUPLE. TALK TOGETHER OF WHAT WILL KEEP YOU FROM HAVING "GIVERS' REMORSE."

BACKGROUND

The Bible has much to say about money. We need clear, biblical guidelines for the uses of the money God has entrusted to us. When it comes to money most people think only about getting it. There is another whole side to our money: giving it. In fact, there is great ministry expressed through giving money. Today's study will list and develop three principles for giving.

PRINCIPLES OF GIVING

READ

1 CORINTHIANS 16:1–4
(FOCUS ON 16:2)

QUESTIONS FOR INTERACTION:

1 Principle #1: Giving is planned. Why do you suppose Paul said to take the first day of the week for determining our giving?

2 Principle #2: Giving is personal. What advantages might there be to giving as an individual responsibility?

3 Principle #3: Giving is proportional. What does it mean to "set aside a sum of money in keeping with his income" (v. 2)? (Give examples from income sources: e.g., payrolls, contracts, commissions, farming.)

4 Paul was concerned that no collections be taken in Corinth. Why?

JESUS SPOKE MORE ABOUT OUR RELATIONSHIP WITH OUR POSSESSIONS THAN HE DID ABOUT BAPTISM, HIS SECOND COMING, HELL, COMMUNION, AND THE BIBLE—ALL PUT TOGETHER.

WRAP-UP: TALK TOGETHER ABOUT THE BENEFITS TO A CHURCH THAT ADOPTS THE GIVING PRINCIPLES OUTLINED IN THIS PASSAGE.

 LET'S PRAY: (SEE PRAYER JOURNAL)

• •

> ### MY RESPONSE AS A PROMISE KEEPER
>
> **1** I will personally evaluate my giving to the Lord's work.
>
> **2** I will begin planned and proportional giving to the Lord's work.

CENT$ APPEAL

WARM-UP: ALAN IS AMAZED AT HOW MUCH MAIL HE RECEIVES EVERY WEEK ASKING FOR FINANCIAL GIFTS. IN FACT, THE EVENING MEAL IS OFTEN INTERRUPTED BY TELEPHONE CALLS WITH THE SAME KINDS OF REQUESTS TO FUND WORTHY CAUSES. AFTER REACTING TO SO MANY FINANCIAL APPEALS, ALAN IS LOOKING FOR A FEW GOOD GUIDELINES TO HELP HIM KNOW HOW TO TARGET HIS GIVING. TALK TOGETHER HOW YOU WOULD ADVISE ALAN.

BACKGROUND

There are many ways we can have a ministry. One of the most common ways is by giving our money. Whether it be contributing to the church collection plate or direct-mail fund appeals, we likely need some guidelines. In today's study, we will learn how to target our giving from three biblical sources.

READ

1 JOHN 3:14–18; 2 THESSALONIANS 3:6–13; GENESIS 42:18–25

QUESTIONS FOR INTERACTION:

1 How does John help us determine to whom we should give? 1 John 3:14–18

2 How does Paul help us determine to whom we should not give? 2 Thessalonians 3:6–13

WALK
WORK
RELATIONSHIPS
MINISTRY

TARGETS FOR GIVING

PK PROMISE KEEPERS®
MEN OF INTEGRITY

3 Why was giving to his brothers such a compelling gesture by Joseph?
Genesis 42:18–25

4 What long-term effect did Joseph's financial gift have upon his family?

WRAP-UP: IF THIS GROUP WERE TO CHOOSE TARGETS OF NEED FOR FINANCIAL GIFTS, TALK TOGETHER ABOUT WHO OR WHAT THAT MIGHT BE. WHY? WHEN? HOW MUCH?

LET'S PRAY: (SEE PRAYER JOURNAL)

• •

MY RESPONSE AS A PROMISE KEEPER

❶ I will pray about my part in our group project.

❷ We will pray to be of one mind about launching this group endeavor.

WINDOWS OF HEAVEN

THIRD IN THE SERIES OF THREE STUDIES: FINANCIAL
PROVISIONS ARE EXPRESSED IN OUR MINISTRY

FINANCIAL ISSUE UNDER CONSTRUCTION: REWARDS OF GIVING

• •

WARM-UP: YOU WOULD NEVER GUESS THAT DAN AND JUDY ARE AMONG THE MOST
GENEROUS GIVERS YOU COULD KNOW. THEY HAVE A MODEST LIFESTYLE,
AND NEITHER OF THEM IS IN A HIGHLY PAID POSITION. THEIR LIVES SEEM
TO BE FILLED WITH CONTENTMENT AND JOY. DAN IS QUICK TO SAY, "SINCE
WE HAVE BEGUN TO GIVE GENEROUSLY, IT IS LIKE THE WINDOWS OF HEAVEN
ARE BEING OPENED ABOVE US." TALK TOGETHER ABOUT WHAT MIGHT BE
FALLING FROM THE WINDOWS OF HEAVEN UPON THEIR LIVES.

BACKGROUND

This chapter, addresses
money issues. The
apostle Paul, concerned
for the poverty-stricken
Christians in Jerusalem,
is encouraging these
believers to give
generously. We find him
using a variety of
motivations to stir their
interest in giving. Today,
our study will accent how
the windows of heaven
are opened on those who
give cheerfully.

REWARDS OF GIVING

READ

2 CORINTHIANS 9:1–15

QUESTIONS FOR INTERACTION:

1 Motivating people to give is an art. What do we learn from
the apostle Paul as he begins to motivate these
Corinthians to give?

2 Paul made reference to the law of sowing and reaping.
Why do you suppose he used this common analogy to
motivate the Corinthians to give?

❸ The attitudes of giving can vary. What are some typical giving attitudes? What motivates cheerful giving?

❹ Why do you suppose God chooses to lavishly bless the giving person? What do these blessings often look like?

WRAP-UP:
GENEROUS GIVING MAKES ITS WONDERFUL IMPACT ON BOTH THE GIVER AND THE RECIPIENT. TALK TOGETHER OF EXAMPLES WHERE YOU HAVE SEEN GIVERS' AND/OR RECEIVERS' LIVES REKINDLED DUE TO GENEROUS GIVING.

LET'S PRAY: (SEE PRAYER JOURNAL)

. . . .

MY RESPONSE AS A PROMISE KEEPER

❶ I will examine my attitudes and motives for giving.

❷ Giving opportunities may be closer than I think. I will look for opportunities to give generously.

THE WORD SPOKEN HERE

FIRST IN THE SERIES OF THREE STUDIES:
HOME LIFE IS DEVELOPED IN OUR <u>WALK</u>

HOME LIFE ISSUE UNDER CONSTRUCTION: <u>THE WORD</u>

• •

WARM-UP: TODAY'S SESSION IS THE FIRST IN A SERIES ON <u>HOME LIFE UNDER CONSTRUCTION</u>. ONE OF THE MOST COMMON WORDS IN OUR VOCABULARY IS THE WORD "HOME." <u>EACH OF YOU USE</u> THE WORD "HOME" IN A SENTENCE THAT DESCRIBES ITS PLACE IN YOUR LIFE.

BACKGROUND

For forty years, the nation of Israel had lived in a mobile home, on the move from Egypt toward the Promised Land. Only the Jordan River ran between them and a new home of permanence. In today's study, Moses is addressing the nation. It is his desire that God's Word be spoken. In today's study, let's picture ourselves crowded around Moses getting final words for entry to a new home life.

READ

DEUTERONOMY 6:1–12

QUESTIONS FOR INTERACTION:

1 What words did Moses say must be spoken in Hebrews' homes? Why these words?

2 In what ways were these vital words to penetrate their homes? What were the likely benefits to the people there?

(WALK) ⇨

THE WORD

PROMISE KEEPERS®
MEN OF INTEGRITY

❸ To this very day, religious Jews still memorize these same words (vv. 4–5) and repeat them regularly. What are the vital words within Christianity for doing the same?

❹ Rote memorization is not the only way to speak the Word of God. What are some creative ways for the Word to penetrate our home lives?

WRAP-UP. THINK BACK TO WHEN YOU MEMORIZED PARTS OF THE WORD. TALK TOGETHER ABOUT THIS TIME: WHEN WAS IT? WHY DID YOU DO IT? WHAT WAS ITS VALUE THEN . . . AND NOW?

LET'S PRAY

ONE MINUTE: PRAY SILENTLY ABOUT TODAY'S STUDY
TWO MINUTES: EXPRESS THANKS TO GOD TOGETHER
THREE MINUTES: WRITE IN YOUR PRAYER JOURNAL
FOUR MINUTES: PRAY FOR EACH OTHER

MY RESPONSE AS A PROMISE KEEPER

❶ I will memorize Deuteronomy 6:5.

❷ I will look for ways to express this verse in my daily life.

PRAYERS OFFERED HERE

SECOND IN THE SERIES OF THREE STUDIES:
HOME LIFE IS DEVELOPED IN OUR WALK

HOME LIFE ISSUE UNDER CONSTRUCTION: PRAYER

WARM-UP: BILL'S WOUNDED BUDDY LAY IN THE MIDDLE OF THE DMZ, CRYING OUT FOR HELP FROM HIS PLATOON. HIS SERGEANT, WHO HAD FOUGHT IN THIS KOREAN CONFLICT FOR SOME TIME, KNEW IT WOULD BE SUICIDE FOR ANYONE TO GO AFTER HIM. BILL KEPT LOOKING AT HIS WATCH WHILE LISTENING TO HIS BUDDY. WITH ONE LAST LOOK AT HIS WATCH, HE JUMPED UP, RACED INTO THE OPEN, AND DRAGGED HIS BUDDY BACK BEHIND THE LINES. HIS INFURIATED PLATOON LEADER YELLED, "WHY DID YOU GO AFTER HIM? WHAT'S THE DEAL WITH CHECKING YOUR WATCH?" BILL REPLIED CONFIDENTLY, "SIR, I WAITED UNTIL 9:00 BACK HOME IN KANSAS BEFORE I MADE MY MOVE. MY MOTHER ALWAYS PRAYS FOR ME AT 9:00." TALK ABOUT WHO COMES TO MIND WHEN YOU THINK OF SOMEONE IN YOUR HOME LIFE WHO HAS PRAYED FOR YOU OVER THE YEARS.

BACKGROUND

The book of Acts chronicles the first few decades of the New Testament church in the Roman Empire. It is not the record of grand cathedrals being built, but rather the stories of individuals and homes being transformed by Jesus Christ. Today's session tells an amazing story of faith amid the fires of opposition.

(WALK) ⇨

PRAYER

READ

ACTS 12:1–19

QUESTIONS FOR INTERACTION:

1 Why was the church praying so fervently for Peter? What do you suppose Peter was praying?

2 Why do you think Mary's house was chosen for this special time of prayer?

3 How did Peter likely know to go to the house of Mary following his miraculous release?

HARD HAT AREA:

IF YOU HAVE SMALL CHILDREN AT HOME, ACT OUT THIS STORY AS A FAMILY. IT WILL BRING REAL LIFE TO YOUR HOME LIFE.

4 We often wonder if we have strong enough faith for our prayers to be effective. Discuss the faith level in the prayer gathering at Mary's home.

WRAP-UP: TALK TOGETHER ABOUT WHAT WOULD BE NEEDED IN ORDER FOR OUR HOMES TO BE KNOWN AS "HOUSES OF PRAYER." WHAT WOULD SURELY BE SOME BENEFITS TO OUR HOMES?

 LET'S PRAY: (SEE PRAYER JOURNAL)

MY RESPONSE AS A PROMISE KEEPER

❶ I will assess my home as a place of prayer.

❷ Whenever a few friends are in my home, I will include a time of prayer.

FORGIVENESS FOUND HERE

THIRD IN THE SERIES OF THREE STUDIES:
HOME LIFE IS DEVELOPED IN OUR WALK

HOME LIFE ISSUE UNDER CONSTRUCTION: CONFLICT

• •

WARM-UP:

WE MAY CONSIDER OUR HOMES AS PLACES OF FORGIVENESS. HOWEVER, BEFORE WE GIVE MUCH MEANING TO THIS THOUGHT WE MUST BE ABLE TO <u>FINISH THESE TWO SENTENCES</u> (FINISH AS A GROUP):

FORGIVENESS IS_____.

FORGIVENESS IS NOT_____.

BACKGROUND

Commonplace to life in the city is the presence of homeless people. Some are on the streets because this place is better than their homes. Others would likely go home if they could. Today's session has become one of Jesus' most memorable stories because He shows the way home from the streets.

READ

LUKE 15:11–24

QUESTIONS FOR INTERACTION:

❶ Describe what might have been the home life of these two sons growing up together.

❷ After the horror of his homeless experience, what brought the prodigal son home?

CONFLICT

PROMISE KEEPERS®
MEN OF INTEGRITY

3 How could the father receive such a worthless and wasteful family member back into his home?

4 Upon his return, the worthless son put together a statement of repentance. Was this necessary? Why/ Why not?

WRAP-UP: THERE MAY BE SOMEONE IN YOUR HOME OR EXTENDED FAMILY WHO NEEDS THE KIND OF FORGIVENESS FOUND IN THIS STORY. REFLECTING ON TODAY'S SESSION, <u>TALK ABOUT</u> WHAT MIGHT BE INVOLVED.

LET'S PRAY: (SEE PRAYER JOURNAL)

MY RESPONSE AS A PROMISE KEEPER

❶ I will ask each member of my household, "Do you think this home is a place of forgiveness?"

❷ Since forgiveness begins in the heart, I will pray the psalmist's prayer, "Search me, O God, and know my heart" (Ps. 139:23).

LATE AGAIN

● ●

WARM-UP:

WE WOULD WISH IT DIFFERENT, BUT OUR HOME LIFE IS EXAMINED IN OUR WORK LIFE. WHEN THE PROMISE BUILDERS GROUP CAME TO THEIR PRAYER JOURNAL TIME, LARRY'S REQUEST FOR PRAYER WAS FOR A TOUGH DECISION CONCERNING AN EMPLOYEE. "I HAVE AN EMPLOYEE WHO IS CHRONICALLY LATE. WHEN I REMINDED THIS PERSON THAT I CANNOT RUN A BUSINESS THIS WAY, MY EMPLOYEE BURST OUT WITH, 'IF YOU KNEW WHAT WAS GOING ON AT HOME YOU WOULD BE MORE UNDERSTANDING!' WHAT DO YOU THINK I OUGHT TO DO?" TALK TOGETHER REGARDING WHAT COUNSEL YOU WOULD GIVE LARRY.

BACKGROUND

We will meet today a man whose professional life was jeopardized by his home life. His profession happened to be the priesthood and his family happened to include two sons and a foster child. We might think he would have a model home. In fact, it was just the opposite. No matter the profession, we pay a high price at work when our home life is unraveling.

UNRAVELED

PROMISE
KEEPERS®
MEN OF INTEGRITY

READ

1 SAMUEL 2:12–26; 3:10–14

QUESTIONS FOR INTERACTION:

1 Samuel, the foster child, wants to send his mom a letter about his new home. What might he write about Eli and his sons?

2 Home life problems like this don't happen overnight. Observing the father-sons interaction (2:22–25), why weren't they connecting?

❸ If you were Eli's employer, how would you speak to his deteriorating work situation? What, in fact, did Eli's Employer do?

❹ "Look, I work seventy hours per week to provide for my family. What more do you want me to do?" Talk together about how you would answer this friend's frustration.

WRAP-UP: GO AROUND THE GROUP AND HAVE <u>EACH PERSON DESCRIBE</u> ONE THING HE IS DOING TO ENSURE THAT HIS HOME LIFE IS HAVING A POSITIVE INFLUENCE ON HIS WORK LIFE.

 LET'S PRAY: (SEE PRAYER JOURNAL)

● ●

MY RESPONSE AS A PROMISE KEEPER

❶ I will recognize that my home life is being examined in my work life.

❷ I will pray for perspective regarding my home life so that it doesn't become a negative factor in my work.

HOME AIR FRESHENER

• •

WARM-UP: HUNTERS KNOW THAT GAME ARE HIGHLY ALERT TO SCENT. IN FACT, A LARGE PART OF A HUNTER'S STRATEGY IS TO STAY DOWNWIND OF HIS TARGET. ALTHOUGH OUR SENSES ARE NOT AS KEEN, WE HUMANS ARE ALSO VERY SENSITIVE TO SCENT. CERTAIN SCENTS TRIGGER MEMORIES. <u>TALK TOGETHER</u> OF VIVID MEMORIES BROUGHT ABOUT BY CERTAIN SCENTS.

BACKGROUND

Whether we like it or not, our home life is inevitably examined in our work. That is, the "scent" of our home life is picked up in our work lives. The Old Testament tells us that sweet, savory sacrifices were given to delight the nostrils of God. The New Testament documents the sacrifice of Jesus on the cross as the ultimate fragrant offering. In today's study, we will discover how to bring a fresh and sweet aroma into our homes and thus to our places of work.

FRAGRANT

READ

EPHESIANS 4:30–5:2

QUESTIONS FOR INTERACTION:

1 If a home is described by verse 31, what aroma do its occupants likely bring to their workplaces?

2 Nobody would question that we should live according to verses 31 and 32. Why is this often so difficult?

3 In a sense, the aroma of our homes reaches to high heaven. How is it that this aroma could hurt the heart of God so deeply (v. 30)?

4 How do the components of 5:1–2 serve to freshen the air in homes?

WRAP-UP: HAVE <u>EACH GROUP MEMBER TELL</u> THE GROUP OF ONE THING WE CAN PRAY ABOUT IN OUR HOME LIVES SO THAT ITS FRAGRANCE WILL BE CARRIED INTO THE WORKPLACE.

 LET'S PRAY: (SEE PRAYER JOURNAL)

MY RESPONSE AS A PROMISE KEEPER

1 I will perform a sniff test to determine if I have an Ephesians 4:31–32 home.

2 I will choose to sweeten the aroma of my home life by _____
_____.

BIG SHOES TO FILL

• •

WARM-UP: "GENTLEMEN, AMONG OUR AGENDA ITEMS FOR THIS EVENING'S ELDER BOARD MEETING IS THE NEED TO TALK ABOUT JAY'S REPLACEMENT ON THE BOARD. HIS SUDDEN MOVE TO PHOENIX HAS LEFT BIG SHOES TO FILL. SINCE WE ARE SITUATED HERE IN THE SUBURBS OF OUR NATION'S CAPITAL, WE HAVE QUITE A LEADERSHIP POOL FROM WHICH TO DRAW. OTHER THAN LEADERSHIP SKILLS, WHAT DO YOU THINK WE SHOULD CONSIDER IN FILLING THIS POSITION?" <u>TALK ABOUT</u> HOW YOU WOULD ANSWER THIS QUESTION.

BACKGROUND

The standards for church leadership are not left up to the consensus of the congregation alone. The New Testament clearly communicates requirements for the one who may take a leadership role. In today's study, we will look for the connection that a person's home life is central in qualifying for the work of leadership in the church.

READ

1 TIMOTHY 3:1–7

QUESTIONS FOR INTERACTION:

1 Having read the list of qualifications for spiritual leadership in the church, which items in the list are not typically required for leadership in the business world?

2 Certainly Paul knew that few, if any, would be able to meet these high standards for church leadership. Why, then, did he set the standards so high?

UNDIVIDED

PROMISE KEEPERS®
MEN OF INTEGRITY

❸ Describe in your own words what a spiritual leader's home life is to be like. Suggest some ways church leaders can help candidates grow toward meeting the qualifications.

❹ Some in this group may presently be in positions of church leadership. Talk together of the benefits to a church when these home life qualifications are met in its leadership.

WRAP-UP: WE HAVE LEARNED THAT CHURCH LEADERSHIP STANDARDS ARE SIMPLY A REFLECTION OF OUR HOME LIFE AND WORK LIFE. HAVE <u>EACH PERSON SELECT</u> ONE ITEM FROM THE LIST OF QUALIFICATIONS IN TODAY'S BIBLICAL SECTION WHEREIN PRAYER IS NEEDED.

LET'S PRAY

PRAY FOR THE PERSON SEATED TO YOUR RIGHT REGARDING THE ITEM HE MENTIONED IN THE WRAP-UP.

· ·

MY RESPONSE AS A PROMISE KEEPER

❶ I will give new value to my leadership at home.

❷ I will seek to be a better manager in my household by _____
_____.

HOME FIRES

● ●

WARM-UP: LOOK AROUND THE GROUP TO SEE WHAT PRECIOUS METALS ARE BEING WORN. TALK ABOUT WHAT YOU KNOW ABOUT THE REFINING PROCESS THAT BRINGS ABOUT SUCH BEAUTY AND QUALITY.

BACKGROUND

A home is to be valued in many ways. It is to be a place of rest, comfort, and warmth. Everyone wants to "keep the home fires burning." Sometimes the home fires are the heat of testing and refining, even as found in the furnace of a goldsmith. We will discover today that the Lord tests hearts, and He often does so in relationships at home.

READ

PROVERBS 17:1-28

QUESTIONS FOR INTERACTION:

❶ Describe the two houses mentioned in verse 1. In what ways are they different?

❷ The king changes the metaphor from refining to waterflow. Why does the king say, "Starting a quarrel is like breaching a dam" (v. 14)? What is both good and bad about inevitable family quarrels?

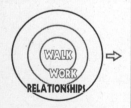

REFINING

3 One of the myths of life is that "I don't need anyone." What has the heat of adversity taught you about this myth (see v. 17)?

4 How does a foolish son or daughter put the heat on a family (v. 25)? How can the Refiner likely use this heat in a family?

WRAP-UP. THE REFINING PROCESS YIELDS GOLD FROM RAW MATERIALS. HAVE <u>EACH PERSON SELECT</u> A WORD OR TWO TO DESCRIBE "GOLD" THAT HAS SURFACED THROUGH THE REFINING PROCESS IN HIM.

 LET'S PRAY: (SEE PRAYER JOURNAL)

• •

MY RESPONSE AS A PROMISE KEEPER

❶ I will identify and thank God for the gold that is appearing in my home life.

❷ I will begin looking for the hand of the Refiner in my home life relationships.

No Place for a Family?

● ●

WARM-UP:

THE MEMORIES OF MEN AND WOMEN WHO HAVE GONE OFF TO A WAR LIKELY INCLUDE THE EXTREME HARDSHIP OF EXTENDED FAMILY SEPARATION. TALK TOGETHER ABOUT WHY MILITARY LEADERSHIP SELDOM PERMITS FAMILIES IN THESE ASSIGNMENTS.

BACKGROUND

One of the greatest undertakings in all of history was the exodus of Israel from Egypt to the promised land. The task of leading more than a million people fell on the shoulders of Moses. Interestingly enough, his family had not been with him since before he left Egypt. In today's study, we will take a close look at the place given to his family. Unlike a military assignment, the family and extended family of Moses join him on the battlefield.

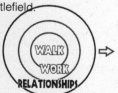

REUNITED

READ

EXODUS 18:1–12

QUESTIONS FOR INTERACTION:

❶ Why do you suppose Moses sent his wife and children back home to her family in Midian?

❷ Imagine Moses' home life and work life after his family left. How might their leaving have benefited him in his overwhelming assignment? How might their leaving have hindered him?

❸ Why do you think Jethro brought his daughter and grandsons back to Moses?

❹ Certainly the relationship between Jethro and his son-in-law was deepened as a result of this visit. Yet what may have been most memorable for Jethro?

WRAP-UP: HAVE EACH GROUP MEMBER CHOOSE ONE OF THESE QUESTIONS TO DISCUSS:
1. DISCUSS WHO IN YOUR EXTENDED FAMILY HAS BEEN LIKE A JETHRO IN YOUR HOME LIFE OR WORK LIFE.
2. DISCUSS WHO IN YOUR EXTENDED FAMILY NEEDS YOU TO BE A JETHRO.

 LET'S PRAY: (SEE PRAYER JOURNAL)

• •

MY RESPONSE AS A PROMISE KEEPER

❶ I will thank my family for their powerful presence in my life.

❷ I will remember to pray for _____ in Promise Builders or my circle of friends whose home life is being tested in relationships.

HOME GROAN

● ●

WARM-UP: A PHENOMENON OF THE NINETIES IS THE BLENDED FAMILY. FIFTY YEARS AGO, PARENTS HAD LOTS OF CHILDREN; TODAY CHILDREN HAVE LOTS OF PARENTS. IN TODAY'S STUDY, WE MEET A MAN WHO IS THE PRODUCT OF THREE HOMES. THE IMPACT OF HIS HOME LIFE BACKGROUND UPON HIS LIFE WAS SUCH THAT HE BECAME ONE OF THE GREATEST LEADERS IN ALL OF HISTORY—HIS NAME IS MOSES. RECALL TOGETHER WHAT YOU MIGHT HAVE READ ABOUT HIS THREE HOMES.

BACKGROUND

It is inevitable that we reflect into all of our relationships the training and influence of our home life. In today's study, we find Moses surrounded by over a million desert travelers. He is likely exercising his leadership through the filters of forty years in Pharaoh's household along with another forty years in his father-in-law's home in Midian. Certainly a man of his age and experience would be a capable leader.

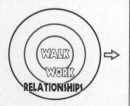

REORGANIZED

READ

EXODUS 2:11–22

QUESTIONS FOR INTERACTION:

❶ What can we learn about Moses' home life in Egypt from the way he related to the men and women in this narrative?

❷ What did Reuel (Jethro) likely see in Moses' character that propelled him to make this stranger his son-in-law?

3 From what sources do you suppose Moses got the idea that he had to lead these people all by himself? Why did his father-in-law say, "What you are doing is not good" (Exodus 18:17)?

4 Discuss why you think Moses did not respond to his father-in-law with, "Look, I have had the burning bush experience with God. Why should I listen to you?"

WRAP-UP: MOSES WAS GIVEN INDISPENSABLE MANAGEMENT PRINCIPLES BY JETHRO. DISCUSS TOGETHER SOME OF YOUR MANAGEMENT PRINCIPLES AND FROM WHOM YOU LEARNED THEM.

 LET'S PRAY: (SEE PRAYER JOURNAL)

● ●

MY RESPONSE AS A PROMISE KEEPER

1 I will take a look back on how my work values have been influenced by my home life.

2 I will be reminded of the power of my home as a teacher of values.

TABLE TALK

● ●

WARM-UP: ALL OF US HAVE HAD THE OCCASION TO BE IN SOMEONE'S HOME FOR DINNER, A HOLIDAY PARTY, OR SOME KIND OF SOCIAL EVENT. OFTEN WHEN WE LEAVE SUCH AN OCCASION WE SAY TO ONE ANOTHER, "WASN'T IT WONDERFUL TO BE IN THEIR HOME!" DISCUSS TOGETHER ABOUT WHAT IN THIS HOME LIKELY MADE FOR SUCH A GOOD TIME.

BACKGROUND

As the early church grew, so did its need to take care of an increasingly diverse group of people. In particular, the Hellenistic (Greek) widows raised a complaint against the largely Jewish leadership. To address this problem, the twelve apostles wisely selected seven Greek men to fill this need. In our session today, we will discover how the home life of one of these men was expressed in his ministry.

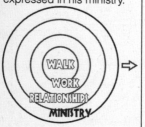

SERVING

MEN OF INTEGRITY

READ

ACTS 6:1-7;
21:8-9

QUESTIONS FOR INTERACTION:

1 The issue at hand for the leadership in Jerusalem was a simple one: serving meals to the Greek widows. Why should such high standards be required for such a simple job?

2 If we could have visited the homes of Philip and his six colleagues prior to being selected to such honorable positions, what might we have observed?

3 Some time later, Paul the apostle and his traveling companions made sure their itinerary included a stop in Caesarea. Why?

4 The children in Philip's home were apparently attracted to serving the Lord. What have you seen and learned that encourages this kind of response among children?

WRAP-UP: PHILIP THE EVANGELIST BEGAN AS A TABLE-SERVER. TALK TOGETHER ABOUT THE "TABLE-SERVING" OPPORTUNITIES THE LORD IS GIVING TO YOU NOW.

 LET'S PRAY: (SEE PRAYER JOURNAL)

● ●

MY RESPONSE AS A PROMISE KEEPER

❶ I will attach new meaning to being a servant at home.

❷ I will see my workplace service as an extension of my home life.

An Officer and a Gentleman

SECOND IN THE SERIES OF THREE STUDIES:
HOME LIFE IS EXPRESSED IN OUR MINISTRY

HOME LIFE ISSUE UNDER CONSTRUCTION: COMPASSION

● ●

WARM-UP: WHEN WE LOOK BACK ON THE DAYS OF OPERATION DESERT STORM, IT IS LIKELY ONE OFFICER COMES TO MIND MORE THAN ANY OTHER. WE ARE STILL HEARING STORIES OF SUCH HIGH REGARD GIVEN TO THIS OFFICER THAT MANY OF HIS TROOPS HAVE SINCE NAMED THEIR SONS AFTER HIM. TALK TOGETHER ABOUT WHAT DISTINGUISHES OFFICERS LIKE GENERAL H. NORMAN SCHWARZKOPF.

BACKGROUND

An officer in the Roman army was an unlikely candidate to model the qualities of life Jesus hoped to find in Israel. He met this gentleman in Capernaum, a Roman outpost on the north shore of the Sea of Galilee. Being a centurion, he was in command of a one-hundred-man fighting unit. In today's study, we meet a man who was an officer and a gentleman.

COMPASSION

READ

MATTHEW 8:5–13

QUESTIONS FOR INTERACTION:

❶ This passage shows a military officer displaying compassion and faith. Which comes first? Why?

❷ Why does Jesus compliment the centurion on his great faith when all he did was respond to the need of his servant?

3 It is commonplace for some to try to separate their home life from their work life. Do you suppose the centurion did this? Why/Why not?

4 In the midst of Jesus' commendation of the centurion's faith and compassion, He makes a shocking statement (vv. 11–12). Whom do you suppose He is addressing, and why?

 WRAP-UP: WHEN YOU SEE A SEVERE AND UNKIND PERSON AT WORK, WHAT IS LIKELY TRUE OF THIS PERSON'S HOME LIFE? <u>TALK TOGETHER</u> ABOUT HOW YOU WOULD HELP THIS PERSON'S LIFE BECOME MORE COMPASSIONATE.

LET'S PRAY: (SEE PRAYER JOURNAL)

MY RESPONSE AS A PROMISE KEEPER

1 I will recognize that compassion in my workplace must begin at home.

2 I will look for opportunities to display compassion to _____.

WELCOME HOME

THIRD IN THE SERIES OF THREE STUDIES:
HOME LIFE IS EXPRESSED IN OUR MINISTRY

HOME LIFE ISSUE UNDER CONSTRUCTION: HOSPITALITY

● ●

WARM-UP:
HOMETOWN MEMORIES MAY BRING TO MIND PICTURES OF AN AIRPORT, A HARDWARE STORE, RESTAURANTS, AND A HIGH SCHOOL—ANY NUMBER OF THINGS. TALK TOGETHER OF WHY A HOMETOWN MAKES US FEEL "WELCOME HOME."

BACKGROUND

READ

LUKE 10:38-42

In this series, we are discovering that our homes can be places of significant service. When we walk with Jesus through the Gospels, we generally find the homes of His friends ministering to Him. One particular home became special to Him. He visited there often. In today's session, Jesus is welcomed in Bethany on the evening of one of His busiest days recorded in the Gospels.

QUESTIONS FOR INTERACTION:

❶ Given what you know about the busy life of Jesus, what likely were His thoughts about going to Bethany?

❷ Jesus was welcomed when He came to Bethany. What did each sister do to make Him feel that way?

HOSPITALITY

PROMISE
KEEPERS®
MEN OF INTEGRITY

3 What was Martha's idea of hospitality? What was Mary's idea of hospitality? Why do you think Jesus placed more value on one than the other?

4 For most of us, being hospitable is neither simple nor effortless. What can we learn from this story to help us?

WRAP-UP.
WHAT BENEFITS LIKELY CAME TO THIS BETHANY HOME BECAUSE IT WAS A PLACE OF HOSPITALITY? DISCUSS TOGETHER WHAT BENEFITS WILL COME TO OUR HOMES WHEN WE PRACTICE HOSPITALITY.

 LET'S PRAY: (SEE PRAYER JOURNAL)

MY RESPONSE AS A PROMISE KEEPER

1 I will review what our family has done to make our home a place of ministry.

2 I will answer this question: What steps can my family and I take to become more hospitable?

CHRISTMAS CHARACTER

A SPECIAL SESSION FOR CHRISTMAS

CHARACTER TRAIT UNDER CONSTRUCTION: GRACE & TRUTH

• •

WARM-UP: BILL AND CAROL DAVIS ARE EXPECTING THEIR FIRST CHILD IN A MONTH. THEY HAVE SPENT MANY EVENINGS REFLECTING ON POSSIBLE NAMES FOR THEIR NEWBORN. THE NURSERY IS READY AND FURNISHED; GRANDMA'S PLANE TICKETS ARE IN THE MAIL; AND BILL HAS REQUESTED VACATION DAYS. TALK TOGETHER ABOUT WHAT THE DAVISES LIKELY HOPE WILL BE THIS NEW CHILD'S CHARACTER QUALITIES.

BACKGROUND

"What child is this, who, laid to rest, On Mary's lap is sleeping?

Whom angels greet with anthems sweet, While shepherds watch are keeping?

This, this is Christ the King, Whom shepherds guard and angels sing:

Haste, Haste to bring Him laud, the Babe, the son of Mary."

In today's special Christmas session, we will focus on two character qualities of Jesus that serve as models for all of us.

GRACE & TRUTH

READ

1 JOHN 1:1–18

QUESTIONS FOR INTERACTION:

❶ Grace and truth were very important to God the Father when He introduced His Son to the world. Why do you think He selected these two qualities?

❷ What will a child be like if raised by parents imbalanced on the side of grace? On the side of truth?

PK PROMISE KEEPERS® MEN OF INTEGRITY

3 Our heavenly Father wants to raise us with grace and truth. Discuss what our lives can be like with this wonderful balance.

 WRAP-UP: IF YOU COULD UNWRAP A GIFT FROM GOD THIS CHRISTMAS—A GIFT CONTAINING ONE CHARACTER QUALITY CONSIDERED IN OUR SESSIONS THIS QUARTER—WHICH WOULD YOU CHOOSE? HAVE <u>EACH PERSON SELECT</u> ONE FROM THE LIST BELOW AND TELL WHY.

SOLID FOUNDATION	COMMITMENT	PURITY
GIVING RESPECT	GODLINESS	GIVING DIGNITY
CONTENTMENT	PASSION FOR GOD	GOOD REPUTATION
HEART FOR PEOPLE	WORKING HARD	COMPASSION

HAVING WALKED WITH CHRIST FOR ANOTHER YEAR, WHAT NEW INSIGHTS CAN EACH OF YOU DECLARE ABOUT HIS GRACE AND TRUTH AT THIS CHRISTMAS SEASON?

LET'S PRAY:

As you pray today, seek to relate your prayers to the Christmas season.

IN THIS SEASON . . .

I will thank God for His grace and truth in my life.

Promise Builders

Date	Prayer Request	From	Answer
6/7/99	Ritchie é Virgina		
	up coming surgery		
6/7/99	Lucy – Results neg.		
7/12/99	Julie King – crack addiction		

PROMISE BUILDERS

PRAYER JOURNAL

DATE	PRAYER REQUEST	FROM	ANSWER

PROMISE BUILDERS

DATE	PRAYER REQUEST	FROM	ANSWER

PROMISE BUILDERS

PRAYER JOURNAL

DATE	PRAYER REQUEST	FROM	ANSWER

PROMISE BUILDERS

PRAYER JOURNAL

DATE	PRAYER REQUEST	FROM	ANSWER

PROMISE BUILDERS

PRAYER JOURNAL

DATE	PRAYER REQUEST	FROM	ANSWER

PROMISE BUILDERS

PRAYER JOURNAL

DATE	PRAYER REQUEST	FROM	ANSWER

PROMISE BUILDERS

PRAYER JOURNAL

DATE	PRAYER REQUEST	FROM	ANSWER

PROMISE BUILDERS

PRAYER JOURNAL

DATE	PRAYER REQUEST	FROM	ANSWER

PROMISE BUILDERS

PRAYER JOURNAL

DATE	PRAYER REQUEST	FROM	ANSWER

Promise Builders

DATE	PRAYER REQUEST	FROM	ANSWER

PROMISE BUILDERS

DATE	PRAYER REQUEST	FROM	ANSWER

PROMISE BUILDERS

PRAYER JOURNAL

DATE	PRAYER REQUEST	FROM	ANSWER

PROMISE BUILDERS

DATE	PRAYER REQUEST	FROM	ANSWER

PROMISE BUILDERS

DATE	PRAYER REQUEST	FROM	ANSWER

PROMISE BUILDERS

PRAYER JOURNAL

DATE	PRAYER REQUEST	FROM	ANSWER

PROMISE BUILDERS

PRAYER JOURNAL

DATE	PRAYER REQUEST	FROM	ANSWER

PROMISE BUILDERS

DATE	PRAYER REQUEST	FROM	ANSWER

PROMISE BUILDERS

PRAYER JOURNAL

DATE	PRAYER REQUEST	FROM	ANSWER

PROMISE BUILDERS

PRAYER JOURNAL

DATE	PRAYER REQUEST	FROM	ANSWER

PROMISE BUILDERS

DATE	PRAYER REQUEST	FROM	ANSWER

PROMISE BUILDERS

PRAYER JOURNAL

DATE	PRAYER REQUEST	FROM	ANSWER

PROMISE BUILDERS

DATE	PRAYER REQUEST	FROM	ANSWER

PROMISE BUILDERS

PRAYER JOURNAL

DATE	PRAYER REQUEST	FROM	ANSWER

PROMISE BUILDERS

PRAYER JOURNAL

DATE	PRAYER REQUEST	FROM	ANSWER

PROMISE BUILDERS

PRAYER JOURNAL

DATE	PRAYER REQUEST	FROM	ANSWER

PROMISE BUILDERS

PRAYER JOURNAL

DATE	PRAYER REQUEST	FROM	ANSWER

PROMISE BUILDERS

DATE	PRAYER REQUEST	FROM	ANSWER

PROMISE BUILDERS

PRAYER JOURNAL

DATE	PRAYER REQUEST	FROM	ANSWER

ADDITIONAL RESOURCES

AVAILABLE FROM PROMISE KEEPERS

PERIODICALS & STUDY TOOLS

BROTHERS! CALLING MEN INTO VITAL RELATIONSHIPS
Geoff Gorsuch and Dan Schaffer (Denver: Promise Keepers, 1993)

DAILY DISCIPLINES FOR THE CHRISTIAN MAN
Bob Beltz (Colorado Springs, Colo.: NavPress, 1993)

FOCUSING YOUR MEN'S MINISTRY
Peter A. Richardson (Denver: Promise Keepers, 1993)

MAKING OF A GODLY MAN
John Trent, Ph.D. (Nashville: Word Publishing, 1997, 1999)

PROMISE BUILDERS STUDY SERIES:

APPLYING THE SEVEN PROMISES
Bob Horner, Ron Ralston, David Sunde (Nashville: Word Publishing, 1996, 1999)

PROMISE KEEPER AT WORK
Bob Horner, Ron Ralston, David Sunde (Nashville: Word Publishing, 1996, 1999)

CHARACTER UNDER CONSTRUCTION
Bob Horner and David Sunde (Nashville: Word Publishing, 1999)

SEVEN PROMISES OF A PROMISE KEEPER
Gregg Lewis (Nashville: Word Publishing, 1999)

STRATEGIES FOR A SUCCESSFUL MARRIAGE: A STUDY GUIDE FOR MEN
E. Glenn Wagner, Ph.D. (Colorado Springs, Colo.: NavPress, 1994)

WHAT GOD DOES WHEN MEN PRAY
William Carr Peel (Colorado Springs, Colo.: NavPress, 1993)

WHAT MAKES A MAN? & STUDY GUIDE
Bill McCartney (Colorado Springs, Colo.: NavPress, 1992)